NEW ENGLAND'S HAUNTED ROUTE 44

THOMAS D'AGOSTINO AND ARLENE NICHOLSON

Haunted America

Published by Haunted America
A Division of The History Press
Charleston, SC
www.historypress.com

Photography by Arlene Nicholson except where otherwise noted.

First published 2023

Manufactured in the United States

ISBN 9781467152129

Library of Congress Control Number: 2023934834

Notice: The information in this book is true and complete to the best of our knowledge. It is offered without guarantee on the part of the author or The History Press. The author and The History Press disclaim all liability in connection with the use of this book.

CONTENTS

ACKNOWLEDGEMENTS

Special thanks to Greenville Public Library, Tavern on Main, Brown & Hopkins General Store, Stone Mill Antiques, Tom Sanzi, Town Trader Antiques, Christopher Balzano, Jim Ignasher, Spooky Southcoast, Matt Moniz, the Oliver House in Middleborough, Smithfield Preservation Society, Putnam Library, Hartford Historical Society, Georgia F. Perry, New York State Tourism, Huguenot Street Tours, Connecticut Paranormal Research Team, the Shanley Hotel, Wing's Castle, Mike Kinsella of Arcadia Publishing, Bolton Historical Society, Jason Medina and Yonkers Ghost Investigators, Tim Weisberg, the Bradley Playhouse, Hale Homestead, Grill 37 in Pomfret, the Valley Breeze and everyone else who helped in the making of this book but wish to remain anonymous.

INTRODUCTION

US Route 44 (US 44) is one of the oldest roads in New England. It is an amalgamation of former turnpikes and newer alignments. The highway runs east–west through New England for 106.03 miles (170.64 km) in Connecticut, 26.2 miles (42.2 km) in Rhode Island and 38.4 miles (61.8 km) in Massachusetts, for a total of 170.63 miles or 270.64 km. Its most eastern tip meets Route 3A in Plymouth, Massachusetts, with the western New England terminus at the New York State border, entering New York and continuing onward for approximately 69 miles. In total, Route 44 runs roughly 237 miles, with the western terminus concluding at US 209 and New York State Route 55 (NY 55) in Kerhonkson, New York, a hamlet in the Hudson Valley region.

Since the 1920s, assignments and realignments of routes led to the making of Route 44. As late as 2007, realignments were made in New York State. In Connecticut, Route 44 was aligned from a series of early turnpikes. From North Canaan to New Hartford, the route was known as the Greenwood Turnpike. As the road continued eastward, it became the Talcott Mountain Turnpike and then the Boston Turnpike. As the road neared the Rhode Island state line, it was known as the Pomfret and Killingly Turnpike. These monikers still turn up on occasion when referring to the highway.

In Rhode Island, Route 44 was once known as the West Glocester Turnpike, the Glocester Turnpike, Powder Mill Turnpike and the Taunton and Providence Turnpike. Reassignments and alignments made the former names all but obsolete.

By 1935, the newly designed Route 44 aligned with the old Route 101, which was assigned in 1922, thus completing a four-state thruway for motorists. In 2005, Massachusetts made one more improvement with a freeway realignment to the north of the original surface alignment of US 44 in the towns of Carver and Plymouth. US 44 was rerouted onto the new expressway to run concurrent with Route 3 from the latter freeway's exit 16 (old exit 7). The new freeway ends south at exit 15A (old exit 6A), where US 44 rejoins its former alignment.

The thoroughfare is laced with small villages and larger cities holding many pieces of important history that helped shape the region. There are also many places along the route that are famous for their ghosts and haunts. This book will take the reader across the span of Route 44, acting as a guide to the haunted places.

Travel guides are always a handy source for those who wish to embark on a road trip. This book will be no different, save for the fact that it will give the adventurer an opportunity to visit some of New England's most interesting places in regard to the paranormal. Within these pages, you will also find places to stay and eat along your journey (some, of course, are haunted), other places or events where you can bide your time between stops on your paranormal trek and some interesting historical tidbits that will enlighten or amuse you. The excitement of this writing is that the journey *is* the destination.

Enter the other side of Route 44, where ghosts roam old graveyards, innkeepers still watch over their establishments, asylums still scream with the ghosts of those who were once confined to them, hostels are still tenanted by those who sojourned within their walls many years ago and a host of other strange entities linger, making Route 44 one of the most haunted highways in the country.

From the famous redheaded hitchhiker to the strange incidents and curses that plague the Bridgewater Triangle, Massachusetts certainly has its share of haunts along the highway. In Rhode Island, ancient buildings grace the roadside with history and haunts of their own. Connecticut takes the lion's share of the highway while serving up its own brand of haunts and mysteries. New York is a bit more eccentric in its place names and ghostly inhabitants. Then there are the places just off the beaten path. A few turns off Route 44 will take you to places that will forever be etched into your paranormal memory. All in all, New England's haunted highway laces through thirty-nine New England towns, villages and cities and fourteen of the same in New York, most with a story and at least a few ghosts.

Take a few days to plot out a route and explore the other side of New England's US Route 44. Take a few side roads and absorb some of the most strange and haunted places the region has to offer. We chose to start at Plymouth based on the fact that the town was the birthplace of America and everyone who came after migrated outward. It seems logical to do the same in this book. If you wish to start from New York, just read the book from the back forward. Unfortunately, not every town along the route is represented, although that would be optimal. Perhaps you may find something along the way that makes for a great story in a place others thought to be void of ghosts. If so, let us know; we love to adventure as well and are always looking for haunts that may have slipped through our fingers. You can be assured: Route 44 is full of haunts and legends both known and waiting to be discovered.

CHAPTER 1

MASSACHUSETTS

PLYMOUTH TO SEEKONK, 38.4 MILES (61.8 KM)

Plymouth

Starting in America's Hometown, Route 44 breaks away from Route 3A and begins its westward journey. Plymouth boasts a lot of spirit activity, making it the perfect start for a haunted road trip. In fact, Plymouth is considered one of the most haunted towns in New England. There are many places that harbor stories of ghosts and haunts that have sustained over the centuries. Leyden Street remains the oldest road made by colonists in the United States. A walk around the area of Plymouth Rock and the old burial ground is a must for ghost enthusiasts. There are also night tours available for those who wish to hear firsthand about the haunts of the town by lantern light. Perhaps you may even see one of the town's eternal residents.

North Street in Plymouth is considered by many paranormal investigators to be the most haunted small street in America. House for house, the haunts add up. One of the most active is the Spooner House Museum.

The Spooner house was built in 1749 for widow Hannah Jackson. The first Spooner to occupy the home was Deacon Ephriam Spooner. For the next two hundred years, the Spooner family made it their home, until James Spooner died in 1954. He bequeathed the residence to the Plymouth Antiquarian Society, which turned it into a museum. The museum now showcases many

Spooner House on famously haunted North Street.

original Spooner heirlooms left behind after James's passing. There is also the ghost of a little girl that resides with the antiques in the home.

In 2005, workmen were hired to perform some needed restorations. The door was locked, so they began knocking. Moments later, a little girl in colonial garb answered the door, then silently ran off into an adjacent room. The workmen called the curator, letting him know that they had arrived, but the door had been locked. When the foreman stated that the little girl let them in, the curator grew puzzled and told him that there was no little girl in the house, as it was a museum and always locked. The work crew curiously entered the room the little girl ran into but were taken aback when they found it empty. The only exit was always within their sight, yet the room was vacant.

The ghost is thought to be that of Abigail Townshend, a little girl the Spooner family adopted as their own. The poor girl passed away a few years later at the age of eight from an abscessed gum that caused a deadly infection. She still remains, either not knowing she is deceased or perhaps still trying to live out the childhood she never had.

Abigail is by no means malevolent, just playful and prankish. One night, a woman on one of the ghost tours came face-to-face with Abigail when the little ghost came up to her and touched her on the back of the shoulder. The little girl, dressed in a white robe, told the woman, "I have to go now," and faded away. The group exclaimed that the special effects of the tour

Spooner House alley, where the ghost of a little girl is seen.

really had them going for a moment. The tour guide insisted he did not have any little girl running around in a robe at ten thirty at night trying to scare people. A guest from another tour saw the ghost of Abigail standing by the corner of the house before vanishing into thin air. Abigail is also occasionally seen peering out the windows of the house at passerby.

Abigail may not be the only ghost haunting the Spooner House. James Spooner, the last of his family to occupy the home, was a music lover. Music is sometimes heard coming from the otherwise vacant dwelling, and lights are seen in the upper windows, as if someone is passing by them with a lantern or candle.

The Spooner House is located at 27 North Street, Plymouth, Massachusetts 02360, 508-746-0012. Take Interstate Route 44 East to Court Street (Route 3A). Bear right onto Court Street, then left onto North Street. For more info, go to https://plymouthantiquarian.org/historic-sites/spooner-house/.

Old North Street Tea and Curiosity Shop

This store has opened and closed several times over the past two decades, but the ghosts remain despite who is running it. Patrons have claimed to witness people walk behind showcases but never emerge from the other side. Various antiques and other quaint merchandise have flown off the shelves in front of customers as if saying, "Take me home." One day, a patron got the scare of his life when a license plate hanging on a rack swung at his head, almost hitting him.

All the past proprietors agree that whoever is permanently residing in the building is very fond of guests. In fact, the ghost of a former upstairs tenant is occasionally seen coming down the stairs from the second floor. Jan Williams is the present owner of the shop and an aficionado of ghost stories, as she also runs the Dead of Night Tours in Plymouth. If you visit 31 North Street, do not be shy about inquiring after their ghosts. It is the spirit of the place that makes it so magical. Oh, and you may want to ask about the tours as well.

Trask Museum

According to its website, "The 1829 Trask Museum is no longer a museum due to the Haunting and objects that move." It is now part of the Dead of

Old North Street Curiosity Shop, home of Dead of Night Ghost Tours—and a few ghosts, as well.

The haunted Trask Museum house.

Night Tours in Plymouth and a museum of the macabre. Special tours of the house and the 1725 Taylor House are available only for those who purchase tickets for the Dead of Night tours. Go to http://deadofnightghosttours. com for more details.

Ghosts of Cole's Hill

Cole's Hill was the scene of secret nighttime burials for those who perished in the first year at the Plymouth Colony. The settlers chose to inter their deceased under the cloak of darkness so the Native Americans would not know how many had died, fearing attack if the Native Americans had any idea how few Pilgrims remained alive. They then planted corn to hide the burials. The great sarcophagus at the top of the hill contains the remains of these unfortunate Pilgrims found during archaeological excavations. The spirits of those buried there are occasionally seen wandering around the monument.

Cole's Hill Monument, where the remains of the original settlers rest, but their spirits do not.

Plymouth Light and Cursed Waters

There is no denying the fact that Plymouth has many tales of ghosts and legends. Thorvald, son of Erik the Red and brother of Leif Eriksson, supposedly made camp here in 1004. Thorvald was mortally wounded by an arrow under the armpit and was allegedly buried at Gurnet Point. Many scholars conclude he was killed and buried somewhere near present-day Newfoundland. Either way, he is hailed as the first European to be buried in North America.

Samuel de Champlain mapped the area in 1606. Early records give it the name "Ye Gurnett's Nose," as it resembled the fish of the same name that was abundant in the waters. The first lighthouse was erected in 1769 when John and Hannah Thomas donated land for such use. The original light consisted of two lantern towers on the roof of a house, making it the first twin tower lighthouse in America. John Thomas was lightkeeper from 1769 to 1776 until he became a general and a casualty of the Revolutionary War. Hannah then took over his duties as the first woman lightkeeper in America.

A fort was erected at Gurnet Point, and it is said that when the British frigate *Niger* fired on the fort, a stray cannonball perforated one of the towers while Hannah was on duty. In December 1778, the American brigantine *General Arnold* shipwrecked off the point near Plymouth Rock. The icy waters claimed seventy-two men. The ice floes were so dangerous that no one, including Hannah, could reach the vessel. Night after night, the men were heard from shore, until finally a causeway of ice was created from the mainland and the survivors were rescued. The dead and dying were brought to the old courthouse to be cared for. Those who survived had spent three horrific days in below-freezing temperatures on the slowly sinking wreck. The deceased soldiers were interred on Burial Hill in Plymouth. James Magee, the ship's captain, carried a burden of guilt for the rest of his short life, dying at the age of fifty-one. His last request was to be buried with his crew members in the mass grave on Burial Hill. A monument was placed on the grave site in 1862. Survivors of the shipwreck forever swore that the vessel was cursed for being named after the colonial general who later became a traitor to the revolutionary cause.

In the 1840s, the lights were torn down and the present octagonal lights were put up in their place. There was something not quite right about the lights, something that could not be repaired or removed: it was the ghost of Hannah.

The old courthouse on Leyden and Market Streets where the survivors of the *General Arnold* were taken.

By 1924, the northeast tower was no longer needed and was taken down. In 1998, erosion made it necessary for the light to be moved 140 feet inland from the slowly crumbling bluffs. All this activity had no effect on the spirit that still mans, or "womans," the light.

Even though the light was automated in 1986, Hannah still stays on duty, keeping the harbor safe for seafarers. Caretakers and visitors often feel her presence in the thirty-four-foot tower. People visiting the light have witnessed the ghost of Hannah wandering the grounds and houses. The Plymouth Light is one of the few working lighthouses in New England, meaning guests can stay overnight or even a week and experience what it is like to be a lightkeeper.

A couple once spent a night at the light and later swore Hannah was in their room while they slept. The man woke from his sleep only to witness the misty figure of a woman hovering over his wife. The ghost was young-looking, with long hair draped over her colonial garb. She had a melancholy expression on her face as she stared at the sleeping woman. In an instant, she was gone. Many believe Hannah's ghost remains, eternally waiting for her husband to return to the light.

For those interested in staying at the Plymouth Lighthouse, go to http://www.newenglandlighthouses.net/lighthouses-with-overnight-accommodations.html.

Plymouth Burial Ground

One of the most visited places in Plymouth is Old Burial Hill, where many of the town's founding families lie in repose—mostly. The graveyard sits on the site of what was once Fort Hill, where the Pilgrims erected a meetinghouse and fortress. Many of the graves date to the 1600s, but most are lost, as they were carved from wood or in the form of grave rails. (Grave rails are early markers consisting of two posts staked into the ground with a wooden rail stretched across the top to mark the grave site.) While meandering through the paths, soaking up the history of the burial ground, you might just come across a Victorian couple who occasionally visit the grave of their long-lost daughter. They appear to be very heavyhearted as they wander down the path past the ancient burials before stopping at a certain grave. The grave is that of Ida Elizabeth Spear, who was born on September 19, 1856, and died on January 23, 1860.

The ghosts of Ida's parents, Thomas Spear and Elizabeth Russell Raymond Spear, have apparently never let go of the fact that she is dead and probably do not realize they are as well. The ghostly couple are seen entering the burial yard from Summer Street and floating solemnly up the path to the site of her burial. Witnesses have noted that they are invisible from the knees down. Ida Lizzy Spear is buried behind her sister, Ida Elizabeth. Lizzy was born on June 1, 1865, and died on August 20 in the same year. It was common for parents to use the same name over and over in hopes one of the children would reach adulthood and pass on the family moniker.

Another area of paranormal activity is the monument for the sailors who perished aboard the *General Arnold* in December 1778. Although Captain James Magee survived the ordeal, he requested to be buried with his men when his time came. People report hearing voices and screams near the grave. Some have witnessed the figure of a man they believe to be Captain Magee wandering around the monument.

One of the legends of Plymouth concerns a descendant of the original Mayflower company, Thomas Southward Howland. In the eighteenth century, Howland evicted an old woman who was living in a run-down cabin built on land he owned. The old woman, Mother Crewe, who was thought

The top of Burial Hill.

to be a witch, placed a curse on him: "Make your peace, because you will not live to see another sunset. They'll dig your grave on Burial Hill." Although he did live to see the sunset, the next day, he was thrown from his horse and killed—and yes, he was interred at Burial Hill.

Ghosts continue to roam the graveyard. Most are unknown, yet they seem to linger in this place where history continues to live, one way or another.

John Carver Inn & Spa

If you decide to spend the night in Plymouth, you may want to check in at the John Carver Inn & Spa. With an eighty-foot water slide winding its way through a life-size replica of the *Mayflower* and a whirlpool Jacuzzi built into a replica of Plymouth Rock, the inn is certainly at home in America's hometown. Burial Hill is to the immediate northwest of the inn, but it is the permanent residents of the inn that may make a night's stay a bit more exciting.

The inn was part of an urban renewal project answering a call for a large, family-oriented tourist hotel. It was originally a Holiday Inn but was renamed in the 1970s. Colonial Lantern Tours tell of a legend stating the inn was built on the site of a former house for medical students. Legend says the students took to grave robbing in order to procure cadavers for dissection. If so, that would easily explain why the inn has a reputation for being haunted.

The kitchen is one place where the ghosts like to play pranks. On certain occasions, pans will suddenly fly off the stove, landing several feet away. The third floor seems to be the most haunted. Room 311 is where guests sometimes feel someone breathing down their neck. Room 309 is said to be the most haunted room in the building. The room gives off vibes that make guests and staff feel uneasy while inside the room. One guest went to sleep but was quickly awoken by a presence and the feeling that someone else was tugging her from behind. She got up to go to the room next door where her friend was staying, and the television suddenly turned on by itself. Much to her surprise, her friend had the same experience at the same time, in a whole different room. Paranormal investigators have recorded voices telling them to leave or get out and also cries for help. According to those who have investigated the inn, there are several ghosts permanently residing there.

The inn is located at 25 Summer Street in Plymouth, right next to the burial ground.

The John Carver Inn.

The old Central Fire Station, now Sam Diego's.

Old Central Fire Station/Sam Diego's

No one is saying too much about this building being haunted, but it is on the Plymouth ghost tour agenda. It is also a great place to eat and have a drink. It is surmised that the ghosts may be those of former firefighters, as the pole from the top floor to the main room downstairs is still present. Take a moment to have a bite to eat and ask about it or book a night tour and learn for yourself the history and haunts of this particular place. Sam Diego's is located on Main Street.

1807: A True Vampire Story

From the late 1700s to the late 1800s, every New England state had a least one documented case of an exhumation and exorcism during what became known as the Vampire Scare of New England. One of the better-known cases concerns an account that took place in Plymouth in 1807. An article appeared in the very first issue of the *Old Colony Memorial and Plymouth County Advertiser* dated May 4, 1822. The author of the article ended the writing with a poem he penned to give the reader a more romantic, yet vivid, recollection of what he actually saw.

In that almost insulated part of the state of Massachusetts, called Old Colony or Plymouth County, and particularly in a small village adjoining the shire town, there may be found the relic[k]s of many old customs and superstitions which would be amusing, at least to the antiquary. Among others of less serious cast, there was, fifteen years ago, one which, on account of its peculiarity and its consequence, I beg leave to mention.

It is well known to those who are acquainted with that section of our country, that nearly one half of its inhabitants die of a consumption, occasioned by the chilly humidity of their atmosphere, and the long prevalence of easterly winds. The inhabitants of the village (or town as it is there called) to which I allude were peculiarly exposed to this scourge; and I have seen, at one time, one of every fifty of its inhabitants gliding down to the grave with all the certainty which characterizes this insidious foe of the human family.

There was, fifteen years ago, and is perhaps at this time, an opinion prevalent among the inhabitants of this town, that the body of a person who died of a consumption, was by some supernatural means, nourished in the grave of some one living member of the family; and that during the life of this person, the body retained, in the grave, all the fullness and freshness of life and health. This belief was strengthened by the circumstance, that whole families frequently fell a prey to this terrible disease.

Of one large family in this town consisting of fourteen children, and their venerable parents, the mother and the youngest son only remained—the rest within a year of each other had died of the consumption.

Within two months from the death of the thirteenth child, an amiable girl about sixteen years of age, the bloom, which characterized the whole of this family, was seen to fade from the cheek of the last support of the heart-smitten mother, and his broad flat chest was occasionally convulsed by that powerful deep cough which attends the consumption in our Atlantick States.

At this time as if to snatch one of this family from an early grave, it was resolved by a few of the inhabitants of the village to test the truth of this tradition which I have mentioned, and, which the circumstances of this afflicted family seemed to confirm. I should have added that it was believed that if the body thus supernaturally nourished in the grave, should be raised and turned over in the coffin, its depredation upon the survivor would necessarily cease. The consent of the mother being obtained, it was agreed that four persons, attended by the surviving and complaining brother should, at sunrise the next day, dig up the remains of the last buried sister. At the appointed hour they attended in the burying yard, and having with much exertion removed the earth, they raised the coffin upon the ground; then, displacing the flat lid, they lifted the covering from her face, and discovered what they had indeed anticipated, but dreaded to declare. Yes, I saw the visage of one who had been long the tenant of a silent grave, lit up with the brilliancy of youthful health. The cheek was full to dimpling, and a rich profusion of hair shaded her cold forehead, and while some of its richest curls floated upon her unconscious breast. The large blue eye had scarcely lost its brilliancy, and the livid fullness of her lips seemed almost to say, "Loose me and let me go."

In two weeks the brother, shocked with the spectacle he had witnessed, sunk under the disease. The mother survived scarcely a year, and the long range of sixteen graves, is pointed out to the stranger as an evidence of the truth of the belief of the inhabitants. The following lines were written on a recollection of the above shocking scene:

> *I saw her, the grave sheet was round her,*
> *Months had passed since they laid her in the clay;*
> *Yet the damps of the tomb could not wound her,*
> *The worms had not seized on their prey.*
> *O, fair was her cheek, as I knew it.*
> *When the rose all its colours there brought;*
> *And that eye,—did a tear then bedew it?*
> *Gleame'd like a herald of thought.*
> *She bloom'd, though the shroud was around her,*
> *Locks o'er her cold bosom wave,*
> *As if the stern monarch had crown'd her,*
> *The fair speechless queen of the grave.*
> *But what lends the grave such a lusture?*
> *O'er her cheeks what beauty had shed?*
> *His life blood, who bent there, had nurs'd her,*
> *The living was food for the dead!*

It is certainly an eerie report of the writer's presumably eyewitness testimony of a family's desperate attempt to affect a cure for the affliction that was taking them, one by one. By turning the body upside down, it was believed, the ghoul would become confused and start digging deeper into the earth instead of rising out of the grave.

UFOs

UFO sightings are nothing new to New England. In fact, accounts of people seeing strange lights moving about in the sky go back to the early days of the colonies. John Winthrop wrote in his journal, published as *The Journal of John Winthrop 1630–1649*, of a strange light seen in the sky on March 1, 1639.

> *In this year one James Everell, a sober, discreet man, and two others, saw a great light in the night at Muddy River. When it stood still, it flamed up, and was about three yards square; when it ran, it was contracted into the figure of a swine: it ran as swift as an arrow towards Charlton, and so up and down about two or three hours. They were come down in their lighter about a mile, and, when it was over, they found themselves carried quite back against the tide to the place they came from. Divers other credible persons saw the same light, after, about the same place.*

In 1808, Cynthia Everett, a twenty-four-year-old Massachusetts native, witnessed a strange light in the sky while in Camden, Maine. As recorded on the *Strange Maine* blog, on July 22, she wrote in her journal:

> *About 10 o'clock I saw a very strange appearance. It was a light which proceeded from the East. At the first sight, I thought it was a Metier, but from its motion I soon perceived it was not. It seem to dart at first as quickly as light; and appeared to be in the Atmosphere, but lowered toward the ground and kept on at an equal distance sometimes ascending and sometimes descending. It moved round in the then visable Horison, (it was not very light) and then returned back again, nor did we view it till it was extinguished.*

Both examples are recorded before the advent of airplanes or other such flying machines. Such lights in the sky could not have been caused by settlements in a region lit by candlelight, rushlight, pine knots and tallow. Such sightings were rare, but then something happened in 1947 that sparked a rash of UFO sightings and caused the government to create a special branch to investigate and log such sightings.

According to Wikipedia, "Project Blue Book was the code name for the systematic study of unidentified flying objects by the United States Air Force from March 1952 to its termination on December 17, 1969."

NEW ENGLAND'S HAUNTED ROUTE 44

The Wright-Patterson Air Force Base in Ohio was the sector's main headquarters. The goals of the project were mainly to "determine if UFOs were a threat to national security and to scientifically analyze UFO-related data." From 1947 to 1969, a total of 12,618 sightings were reported. Of these, 701 remain "unidentified." The results of this work have since been released to the public and can be borrowed from libraries or purchased for perusal.

MUFON took over where Project Blue Book left off. The all-volunteer organization officially began on May 31, 1969. At that time, it was known as the Midwest UFO Network. As it outgrew the Midwestern state boundaries to become a world-class UFO organization, its name was changed to Mutual UFO Network. Today, it ranks as the oldest and largest investigative organization for UFOs and the like in the world. It has over four thousand active members and a file load of over one hundred thousand cases.

Traveling through the towns and cities along Route 44 may just take you into another realm, the extraterrestrial world of UFOs. There are many accounts of UFO sightings in the last one hundred years along New England's haunted highway. Included in this book are some of the more prominent cases that attracted the attention of the government enough for it to log them in its files.

There are many reported sightings along the Route 44 corridor that gained the attention of the news and government, starting in Plymouth.

On May 16, 2021, in America's Hometown, Plymouth, Massachusetts, a large, dull white cigar or disc hovered and then gradually glided east, where it vanished into the darkness. Another case took place on May 20, 2017. MUFON labeled it case no. 83881. The witness saw a black, triangular craft moving silently through the sky. It was rather blurry looking, with a white light at each point.

Carver

In Carver, Massachusetts, at midnight on February 4, 2020, a sphere was seen hovering over the cranberry bogs. The sphere stuck around for an hour before disappearing into the night sky.

Old World Fun

For those who wish to transport themselves back in time, Carver is the setting for the famous King Richard's Faire, held every autumn through September and October. It is quite an extravagant affair.

Middleborough/Lakeville: Watchers of the Woods

Assawompsett Pond is the largest body of water in Massachusetts. The pond shares its waters with Long and Pocksha Ponds. Although it is now used as a water supply for almost a quarter million people, it was once a Wampanoag summer campsite. The name translates to "place of white stone," and archaeological digs in the late 1950s uncovered artifacts and a burial ground dating as far back as 2,300 BC.

Although swimming and bathing is forbidden, hiking, fishing, boating and picnicking are allowed in specific parts of the conservation areas. One particular area called Betty's Neck has three miles of trails where visitors can hike, fish, geocache and picnic. This is also the location of an ancient Wampanoag summer campsite. The pond is also where the body of John Sassamon was found on January 29, 1675.

A group of Algonquians stumbled on Sassamon's body floating beneath the ice. At first, his death was believed to be an accident, but as time went by, authorities came to believe he was murdered. Sassamon was a "praying Indian," having converted to Christianity with the help of missionary John Eliot. It was Eliot who also arranged for his education at Harvard University. According to a few eyewitnesses, Sassamon was murdered by his own people for telling the governor of the Massachusetts Bay Colony about an impending attack by the Wampanoags. A trial by the English found the three Wampanoags guilty and sentenced them to death. This event became a main catalyst for the now-famous King Philip's War.

Between the burial ground being disturbed and the murder of Sassamon, it is no wonder the area of Betty's Neck is haunted. Locals claim to see strange, flickering lights in the woods by the pond where the camp was. Some have actually seen apparitions of Indians from long ago appear in the woods and then suddenly disappear right in front of them. Visitors often feel like the woods, or something in the woods, is watching them as they trek the trails.

According to one account, a woman visiting the area heard her child talking to someone, yet no visible person was present. When she asked who the child was speaking with, the youngster answered that "Conanchet" was saying how he used to fish the waters there many years ago.

Go south off Route 44 to Betty's Neck Road and let the adventure begin.

A UFO Sighting

Middleborough, also within the realm of the Bridgewater Triangle, became another site of UFO activity when on August 8, 2018, a small, high-altitude amber light faded to a bright white before vanishing. Another event took place on September 27, 2020, when a dark circle hovered over Route 44 for about two minutes before taking off into the clouds.

Another UFO Sighting

On December 10, 1998, witnesses watched a brightly lit object with red, green and white lights maneuvering over Assawampsett Pond in Middleboro. The object split in two, and the two pieces began doing strange counter-patterns with each other at a high rate of speed. The two components displayed brilliantly colored lights. The two pieces then rejoined and flew off at an incredible rate of speed. Moments later, air force jets were seen combing the sky over the pond.

The Oliver House

One of the most haunted houses along Route 44 is the Peter Oliver house, located at the corner of the highway and 445 Plymouth Street. The home was built in 1769 by the Oliver family as a wedding gift to Dr. Peter Oliver and Sally Hutchinson. Many famous dignitaries of the time visited the home, as the Olivers were one of the wealthiest families in the colonies. It was one of two homes they had in the area. The other, Oliver Hall, was burned by patriots in 1778.

The Olivers, loyalists to the king of England during the revolution, fled to Canada and, eventually, England. The remaining home was confiscated and items sold to help pay for war expenses. The home eventually came back

Above: The haunted Oliver House welcomes paranormal investigation groups to spend time communicating with the ghosts.

Left: Staircase where the ghost of a woman is seen in the Oliver House.

to the family in the 1940s. The building sits on fifty-four acres and is now a museum where tours are held and paranormal investigations are performed for a small fee.

The Oliver home is abundant with spirits from its past. Many people were born and died in the historic structure. Both residual and intelligent spirits have been encountered by countless people. The ghosts of two women roam about the premises. One is thought to be that of Sally Hutchinson Oliver, the first occupant of the house. The ghost of a woman is occasionally seen at the top of the staircase leading to the second floor. This apparition has prompted several paranormal television shows to spend a night at the house in hopes of witnessing her on the stairs.

Disembodied screams, ghostly conversations and even voices interacting with the living are common at the Oliver house. One former owner often left a bottle of whiskey in one of the reading closets for one of the ghosts that was reported to enjoy the libation. One volunteer conducting a tour came face-to-face with a full-body apparition in one of the second-floor bedroom closets. She stated it was a girl who stared at her for a few seconds before disappearing into the wall. The table in the dining room is always set, for a certain number of spirits that like it that way. The staff feels the spirits are appeased by the table being ready for their supper.

Table is set for spirits to dine at the haunted Oliver House.

One of the many haunted rooms in the Oliver House.

Ghosts of men and children have been seen in the house and gardens as well. Reports of fairies or little gremlins reclining in a very old tree out back have also been documented. Some of the permanent residents of the place have been identified by portraits and photos, while others are still unidentified.

Caretaker Christy J. Parrish has seen and heard a lot in the old house. She embraces the ghosts and their tenancy there as a magical experience. The home is available for six- and eight-hour paranormal investigations for up to ten people. Look up the Oliver House in Middleborough, Massachusetts, for more details and information.

Middleborough Town Hall

Many public buildings are haunted by someone who once worked there, whether it was an official or other employee. The town hall in Middleborough seems to have several spirits roaming through its halls. This particular town hall, built in 1873 by Solomon K. Eaton, has served many purposes over its lifetime. It was a library until 1904, a high school from 1873 to 1886, a court for forty years and a bank at one point. With so many hats, it is hard to tell exactly who the ghosts are—except for one, that of Mr. Eaton himself.

Solomon never got to see the finished product he so lovingly designed in life. It was not until death that he ventured into his pride and joy. Footsteps are heard on the ornate staircase, and sounds of a party are heard in the grand ballroom. Noises like items being moved around emanate from the auditorium. When investigated, the room is found to be vacant. Witnesses attest to seeing the apparition of Eaton wandering around as if proud of his design. His mortal remains are buried in the Cushing Cemetery in Mattapoisett with those of his family.

Hand Rock

Hand Rock sits near the site of the former Middleboro fort erected by the colonists. The legend of the rock was born during King Philip's War and has endured for centuries.

For several days in 1675, a small band of warriors was seen roaming the area near the fort on the opposite bank of the Nemasket River. Each day, one of the warriors came forth, standing at the edge of the river and tormenting the colonists inside the fort. It was an effort to provoke an attack, but none of the people in the fort felt an attack was necessary. Instead, they recruited Isaac Howland, an expert marksman, to shoot the tormentor. Howland took aim with his musket and fired, mortally wounding the warrior. It was considered an amazing feat for the time, as the distance was 150 rods or 2,475 feet. This was way beyond the accuracy range of an ordinary musket of the era.

As the warrior died, his handprint became emblazoned in the rock. A shaman later blessed the rock, making it a sacred Native place. Since then, the ghost of the fallen warrior has been witnessed at the rock.

A man walking by the rock with his grandson was surprised to see his grandson waving at someone. When the man inquired about who he was waving to, the boy told him an Indian was standing at the rock, waving back at him. Sometime later, the incident repeated itself when the boy, once again, began waving at the invisible warrior.

Hand Rock is located at Barden Hill off Route 105.

Titicut Conservation Area, Route 44 and 495

Nestled in a patch of woods within the Bridgewater Triangle is an old boys' camp called Titicut. The area was originally used by Indigenous peoples as a summer camp. A native burial ground still lies inside the camp. The camp was allegedly utilized as a boys' camp from the 1930s to the 1950s. During that time, a boy drowned in the pond. His restless spirit is seen and heard in the woods within the camp.

King Philip's body was reportedly drawn and quartered in the vicinity of the camp. Legend states that the sound of the rustling leaves when there is no wind is his body parts trying to locate each other.

The camp did not actually open until 1950, and King Philip was killed, drawn and quartered sixty miles away in Rhode Island. Both are obviously old campfire tales. Camp legends do not have to be accurate, only scary. According to another account, a girl drowned in the river in the 1960s.

"Titicut" in the Wampanoag language translates to "the place of great river." The area is situated in the northwest section of Middleborough. It is a former reservation that was officially deeded to the Wampanoags on June 9, 1664, by Josias Wampatuck, the son of Chickataubut. This deed covered a three-mile-long tract of land along the Taunton River called Cotunicut. The reservation was used as a campsite and burial ground. By 1770, most inhabitants from the reservation had died or moved on.

From 1946 to 1951, archaeological excavations performed by the Massachusetts Archaeological Society turned up over six thousand artifacts and a Wampanoag burial ground. Some of the skeletons showed signs of having been killed by possible raids. In the 1990s, the remains were given to the Mashpee Wampanoag tribe for reburial on their land. The thirty-three-acre camp is now known as Titicut Conservation Area, and very little remains of the original boys' camp.

Hikers still report seeing the ghosts of former tribal men and women within the woods and the ghost of the little boy. Others report the feeling of being watched while walking the trails, and some claim to have seen dark forms darting among the trees. Voices and screams have been reported and even recorded by paranormal investigators attempting to contact the spirits of the forest.

There are several paths leading you through the conservation area. All that remains of the camp is a few firepits, what was once a flagpole and some remnants of a building.

While You Are There: Raynham's Will o' the Wisps

Every January, investigators and legend trippers come to Raynham to see the glowing orbs called spook lights that appear along the old railroad tracks behind the Raynham Park Simulcast Center. The dancing lights appear out of nowhere, then disappear again without a trace. The facility is located on Broadway in Raynham.

Elm Street in Bridgewater is no stranger to these so-called will o' the wisps. These strange orbs of light are randomly seen along the street before mysteriously vanishing. Some have claimed they are nothing more than fireflies, but that is quite impossible, as that particular species of insect is not seen during the winter months.

UFOs, Bridgewater Triangle

Raynham, Massachusetts, lies within the Bridgewater Triangle, where many strange sightings of both creatures and UFOs run rampant.

On April 4, 2020, a UFO circled an area of town for five minutes. The craft had one white, orb-like light as it maneuvered above the trees. Witnesses were convinced it was not a drone of any kind as it was much too large and maneuvered quietly and effortlessly.

Bridgewater, the heart of the famed Bridgewater Triangle, had an encounter with a vehicle from the skies on October 16, 2020. Around seven o'clock one evening, a craft was seen for about six seconds before darting out of sight at a high rate of speed. The UFO had three moving lights in a straight line along its outer skin.

Old Asylum, Taunton

Although most of the asylum buildings were demolished, some are still used by a modern medical facility currently occupying the land. Stories of the asylum, whether true or not, are horrifying, to say the least.

The building was erected in 1854 by renowned architect Thomas Kirkbridge. It was initially called the State Lunatic Hospital at Taunton, and as in other asylums at the time, abuse, neglect and other unspeakable atrocities took place within its walls. Cult activity reportedly took place in the basement of the sanctuary, where patients were used in black rituals.

There were claims that the cult even conjured the devil himself. The facility closed in 1975.

Over time, portions of the hospital were forced to close due to severe neglect. In 1999, the Kirkbridge building dome collapsed, just five years after being put on the National Register of Historic Places. In 2006, some of the buildings were destroyed by fire, and in 2009, more of the complex was demolished for safety reasons. Some of the old buildings remain but are off-limits to the public. Included in the confines of the hospital are the decaying wings of the old Kirkbridge building and some of the newer buildings repurposed for modern use.

Staff members have reported cold spots following them in the basements of the buildings. One staff member experienced the awful sensation of the death and terror that once took place in the lower chamber as he reached the bottom of the stairs. He was so overcome with fear and dread that he quit immediately.

People inside the building experience lights going on and off all the time. Lights will turn on suddenly in the main office at night when it is locked tight. Residents have seen a faceless, shadowy figure in the shape of a man appearing in their rooms or wandering about the corridors of the old sections of the grounds. Former patients from Taunton State were buried in pauper's graves at the Mayflower Hill Cemetery and the St. Joseph Cemetery. Women in the hospital used to sew burial gowns for those who died while in the care of the facility.

The Goss Building has the spirit of a man in white that walks along the corridors of the third floor, and a corner room on that same floor is home to a most unnatural entity. People who enter the room get a severe feeling of fear that envelopes them until they pass the threshold back into the hallway. The woods near the hospital also are haunted by a number of ghosts. Moans can be heard breaking the silence in the dead of night and even low-pitched screams and banging sounds. Some attribute the noises to former patients of the hospital.

The Taunton State Hospital was also home to one of the most prolific serial killers in American history. Jane Toppan was born Honora Kelley in 1857. Jane's mother died when she was very young, and at age six, she was abandoned when her father dropped her and her sister off at the Boston Female Asylum before vanishing from their lives forever. The Toppan family of Lowell took her in as an indentured servant, and she adopted their last name.

Jane Toppan was intelligent but, at the same time, showed the tendencies of a sociopath, a person who exhibits extreme antisocial, sometimes violent, behavior. She trained for nursing at Cambridge Hospital in 1885 and made many friends. She was nicknamed Jolly Jane because of her friendly nature and high spirits—obviously, a persona she adopted to keep her true self a secret.

Toppan began using patients for experiments with morphine and atropine. Not only would she inject patients with lethal doses, but she would also lie in bed with them as they died. She would go on to kill thirty-one patients before turning her killing spree toward others, including her foster sister, Elizabeth Toppan. Toppan's end came when a toxicology report on one of the patients revealed the cause of death: strychnine. Toppan was arrested in 1901, tried and found not guilty by reason of insanity. She was committed to the state hospital, where she spent the rest of her life, dying in 1938.

During an interview with police, she stated her aim was "to have killed more people—helpless people—than any other man or woman who ever lived."

Mayflower Hill Cemetery

A trip to the Mayflower Hill Cemetery will reveal a most interesting legend and alleged haunt. Within the gates sits a grave site with a marble rocking chair perched on a pedestal. Carved into the base are the words, "Her Vacant Chair." The chair is a memorial to Pearl E. French, who was born August 21, 1878, and died on March 26, 1882, presumably from spinal meningitis, at three years of age. A monument for her and other family members, including her cousin, who supposedly suffered the same fate, sits just behind the chair. Her cousin Veva L. Johnson was born on October 28, 1880, and died on April 26, 1884. Both names and dates are on the obelisk facing the chair.

There are several legends associated with this unusual grave site. People claim to see glowing lights floating around the grave at night. Some have sworn they witnessed the chair rocking back and forth as if someone was sitting in it. The sight of the plot itself is a bit unnerving, and knowing that a child presumably haunts it makes it a bit more eerie still. Is Pearl actually occupying the chair, or could it be her cousin rocking back and forth in the dead of night?

Take Route 44 into Taunton Center to the Broadway intersection. The cemetery is not far from the intersection.

The McKinstrey House

The McKinstrey House, built in 1759, is now the rectory for St. Thomas Episcopal Church. The church has owned the property since 1828, but many believe it is haunted by one of its first owners, Dr. William McKinstrey's sister, Elizabeth.

On June 4, 1763, the doctor's sister was killed by a servant named Bristol. Elizabeth was working in the kitchen when Bristol gabbed a flatiron and struck Elizabeth in the head without any known provocation. Elizabeth fell into the open flames in the hearth, burning one side of her face. Bristol then dragged her into the home cellar and attempted to finish her off with an axe. Elizabeth survived the next twenty-four hours before finally succumbing to her brutal injuries.

Bristol fled but was captured in Newport, Rhode Island, where he was tried, convicted of the murder and executed on December 1, 1763. Dr. McKinstrey, being a Tory at the time of the Revolution, attempted to flee to England but died in Boston Harbor of tuberculosis in 1776. In 1779, the Massachusetts legislature confiscated the property, and the church subsequently acquired it.

The spirit of Elizabeth appears to be quite active in the old home. People hear the rustling of an old-fashioned skirt pass by them while in the building. One rector heard dusting outside his room in the small hours of the morning. When he went to check, there was no one. Elizabeth also likes to take items, returning them later to other locations. The rectory is private property, so please obey all laws and regulations.

Elizabeth is buried in the Plain Cemetery on Route 138 in Taunton. The hanging ground where Bristol met his end is just north of the Plain Cemetery between Broadway and Washington Street.

UFOs in Taunton Are Well Documented

In December 1976, a yellowish object was seen landing near Route 44 in Taunton. Investigators went to the scene and saw a field where the brush and grass had been flattened, but the UFO had vanished. On March 23, 1979, two people from WHDH, a television and radio station based in Boston, witnessed a flying object shaped like a baseball home plate hovering at the junction of Routes 24 and 106. The UFO suddenly took off like a rocket into the sky, disappearing from view within seconds. In January 1991, a giant green disc was seen over Bridgewater about fifty feet in the sky. It disappeared behind some trees. In November 1997, Bridgewater law officers witnessed a triangular flying object with three white lights and two red ones flying overhead. No planes or other man-made objects were known to be flying in the area in question.

Holiday Inn: 770 Myles Standish Boulevard Off Route 44

If you are looking for a place to stay while in the area, it may be an easy choice. The Holiday Inn in Taunton is reportedly haunted. Disembodied voices at night and strange, overwhelming feelings are just some of the occurrences at the hotel. The fifth floor is said to be the most active. There are reports of ghostly voices telling guests to leave. The haunting is believed to be caused by two people who allegedly committed suicide in the inn.

Dighton

Along the banks of the Taunton River once stood what is called Dighton Rock. The forty-ton, five-foot-high, almost ten-foot-long glacial boulder has since been moved to a small museum nearby. The rock contains mysterious carvings and petroglyphs of uncertain origin. The inscriptions on the rock have created controversy for hundreds of years. At first, they were thought to be of Norse origin, while others claimed they were Phoenician. When shown the inscriptions in 1789, George Washington debunked the Phoenician theory, stating that he had seen similar inscriptions throughout his travels in Virginia.

The inscriptions were first discovered in 1680 by John Danforth, a Harvard graduate who meticulously made a copy of the unusual symbols and letters. Edmund B. Delabarre proposed in 1912 that the carvings were from the Portuguese explorer Miguel Cortereal (Corte-Real). Manuel da Silva, the author of several interesting books on the rock, found that some of the carvings are in Portuguese. When Delabarre deciphered the inscriptions, he discovered that some may have been from the Portuguese explorer. He proposed that the rock was carved in abbreviated Latin and, when translated to English, read, "I Miguel Cortereal, 1511. In this place, by the will of God, I became chief of the natives."

A Portuguese coat of arms is also carved in the rock. It is a historical fact that Miguel Cortereal disappeared in 1502 while sailing across the Atlantic

Ocean in search of his brother. Their father, João Vas Cortereal, traveled to the new land via Newfoundland in 1472. That was twenty years before Columbus sailed toward the Americas. After viewing the inscriptions on the rock, many scholars believe that Manuel da Silva's and Delabarre's theories seem to hold some validity but not all the carvings are from the same person.

There are Indigenous people's carvings mixed with the Portuguese ones and other carvings of unknown origin, making the rock a primitive canvas for historical graffiti. Also included in the theories is the idea that ancient Chinese sailors may have put their mark on the rock as well. Whether they were following Cortereal's idea in carving on the rock or he was copying theirs is not known. The exact timeline of the carvings is vague, but their origin and purpose are even more of an enigma. Dighton Rock State Park is located on Third Avenue in Berkley. For more info and to schedule a visit, call 508-644-5522.

The Phantom Hitchhiker of Route 44, Rehoboth

One of the most celebrated haunts along Route 44 is the Redheaded Hitchhiker seen along the Rehoboth/Seekonk line. Yes, he is real, and there are plenty of accounts of his appearance along that lonely stretch of road. This thumbing apparition has prompted more legend trips than almost any other ghost along the haunted highway.

The ghost is described as a man about forty years old with a red plaid shirt, blue jeans and thick, somewhat disheveled red hair. Drivers will stop to give him a ride, and sometimes the hitcher will actually get into the car. Other times, the driver will wait for him to catch up to the auto; when they look back to see if he is approaching, no one is there.

AAA has answered reports of cars breaking down along the five-mile stretch only to find a very unnerved operator rambling about a red-headed ghost they just encountered. Some travelers have claimed to hear a burst of insane laughter echoing in the eerie darkness of the wooded tract, slowly rising out of nowhere before surrounding them from every direction, just after witnessing the ghostly hitchhiker. There are some accounts in which drivers came upon the figure on the road so suddenly that there was no time to react. Their automobile passed through the being with no crash or thump. If the motorist pulled over to check out what they just witnessed, they were subjected to the slow, sinister giggle that soon turned into an evil screech. On one occasion, a man passing through the area in question looked out his passenger-side window and saw a face pressed against the glass, which almost scared the life out of him because, at the time, he was traveling about fifty miles an hour.

A person who lives in the area of the Rehoboth/Seekonk line once picked up a hitchhiker while driving home one night. She assumed he had broken down somewhere and got messy trying to fix his automobile. He looked to be in his forties and was dressed rather plainly, with unkempt, floppy red hair. As the Good Samaritan pulled over to let the rider in, she noticed he was not exactly normal in color but attributed the hue to the dark, moonless night. She asked where he was going, and the man smiled and pointed forward. The woman figured he wanted the first service station and began driving. As they drove on, she looked over, attempting to make conversation with the stranger, but became utterly horrified when she saw the passenger seat was vacant. She then realized she had encountered the spirit that wanders the short length of Route 44, waiting for unsuspecting motorists to happen his way.

Paranormal investigators and legend trippers still make the trek out to this remote section of Route 44 in hopes of spotting the ghostly rider and perhaps even having him in their automobile. Every day, countless cars travel that stretch of road, many probably unaware of the legend. Maybe some have seen him and never thought twice or bothered to catch a better glimpse of the man as they pass by.

Who is the ghost that now haunts the road? The identity of the redheaded hitchhiker, for the most part, remains a mystery. No one has been able to put a name to the ghost. One woman who witnessed the apparition researched the area and found out that a local farmer fitting the hitchhiker's description was hit by a car many years ago while changing a flat tire in the same vicinity where the apparition is seen. Maybe the truth stands waiting on the side of the lonely stretch of road that sporadically crosses over into the boundaries of another world.

Anawan Rock

Anawan (Annawan) Rock is a massive boulder just off Route 44 in the woods of Rehoboth. The rock was the site of the last conflict of King Philip's War, the bloodiest war per capita ever fought on American soil. The war for the most part, lasted one year and two months, but random attacks on colonial settlements continued until 1678. Its toll was devastating for colonists and

Indigenous peoples alike. Unlike in most wars, women and children were mercilessly executed on both sides when whole villages were raided. This was a war fought not for power but for revenge and obliteration of a culture.

The critical factor leading up to the war was the murder of "praying Indian" John Sassamon. Sassamon, a liaison between the English and the Natives, was found murdered in Assawompset Pond. Three Wampanoags were arrested, tried, convicted and executed for the deed by the English on June 8, 1675. Chief of the Pokanokets and powerful sachem Metacom—or King Philip, as he was known to the English—became angry over the fact that the English had taken it upon themselves to seek justice for a tribal matter. This set off a chain of events as the tribe retaliated against the English for infringing on their sovereignty. The legend of the rock begins when Chief Annawan chose that area for his encampment during the waning days of the war in 1676. There, he and his band of warriors hid from the colonists' advancements for days, until August 28, 1676, when General Benjamin Church and his men crept over the rock and surprised the unarmed group. This marked the end of King Philip's War and the defeat of the Wampanoag people.

General Church promised that the Wampanoag sachem would not be harmed as a condition of his surrender. The general kept his word, but his colleagues were not so humane. When they reached their destination in Plymouth, the braves were duly executed, and Chief Annawan was beheaded for his role in the uprising. Because of the White man's treachery, many believe, the rock is cursed by those who were betrayed by the magistrates at Plymouth.

Visitors to the rock have witnessed Indian ghosts running about the woods. One visitor to the site heard the word *iootash* screamed at him while on the rock. *Iootash* is an Indian word meaning "stand and fight." It is known that Annawan surrendered without firing a single shot. Their rifles were perched on a stand out of reach when Church and his men came upon them. Perhaps it is the angry spirits in search of restitution. Smoke and flames from a ghostly campfire are sometimes seen on the boulder, even though there is no such fire. Years ago, ghost hunter Courtney Chadwick took a photo of what appears to be smoke rising from the rock where no smoke was at the time the picture was taken. Although no one died at the rock in that siege, many of the souls and spirits that sought refuge there may have returned to protect what they saw as a sacred place in life.

Anawan Rock is located in the woods just off Route 44. Follow the path about fifty yards into the woods; the rock will be right in front of you. A sign marks the parking area for visitors to the rock.

Rehoboth Village Cemetery

The Village Cemetery in Rehoboth, Massachusetts, hosts a most unfriendly ghost—or at least those who have witnessed him seem to think so. Reported sightings of the apparition go back a few decades, but the haunt appears to be of Victorian origin. Those who have witnessed him say he is dressed in period clothing, but he certainly is not affable or courteous like a Victorian. Furthermore, a few of the sightings, as you will soon read, take on a sinister tone.

A couple visiting a relative's burial plot first noticed the older man kneeling near a grave, praying while alternately crying and laughing. At first, they thought he might be visiting a recently deceased person, but as they watched, the figure vanished before their eyes. This incident left the couple reluctant to return to the cemetery, even though it was where their relatives were buried. The couple made haste for the entrance where their automobile was parked.

Two sisters witnessed the ghost while visiting the grave of their mother. The afternoon was clear and pleasant, and they were sure there were no other living beings in the cemetery at the time—or so they thought. Suddenly there came the sound of whistling from the southwest portion of the cemetery. Vulgar remarks and noises accompanied the whistling. They turned and saw an elderly man making obscene gestures with his hands. The man was standing at the rear of the graveyard and appeared to be translucent. His eyes were black and hollow, without life or compassion. He seemed to float rather than walk as he began to move toward them before vanishing into thin air.

Another witness gave an identical description of the ghost, but this time, as she walked through the cemetery for exercise, the entity chased her. At first, she saw him kneeling before a grave, sobbing and laughing simultaneously. The figure suddenly jumped up as she came close to him and broke out in strange laughter. He then began screaming at her, calling her Catherine and shouting obscenities.

The woman began to run toward her car while the man gave chase, still screaming, "Catherine, you ——! When she reached the car, she turned and noticed he was back kneeling at the grave where she first saw him. He had somehow transported himself several hundred feet within a few seconds. This time, she saw him pounding his fists on the form of a woman lying on the ground. In an instant, both figures were gone. Several accounts of this ghost have been penned over the decades, yet no one knows who the older man is or why he is so angry.

Haunts like this one, where the man is seen beating a woman before vanishing, are usually classified as residual. A residual haunting is one in which the earth, being magnetic, tapes a moment in time and replays it when the correct conditions prevail. This man seems to acknowledge the presence of the living, making him a more intelligent haunt. Perhaps it is a mixture of both, one perpetuating the other.

If you decide to visit the cemetery, take a walk to the southwest portion of the grounds, and if you are lucky, you just may get to witness the nasty ghost of the unknown angry man.

While You Are There: The Shad Pond Factory

The Orleans Manufacturing Company, located on the banks of Shad Pond, was created in 1810 by the residents of Rehoboth. It was first called the Palmer's River Manufacturing Company and was built on the site of an old gristmill. In 1826, its name was changed to the Orleans Manufacturing Company, where fine cloth was made from cotton procured from New Orleans. The mill burned down in 1831 but was rebuilt, and production resumed. The outbreak of the Civil War in 1861 put restraints on the shipping of cotton from the South, forcing the company to change its production to the manufacturing of yarn and thread.

In 1884, another fire broke out, burning the factory for the last time. All that is left of the Orleans Manufacturing Company is sections of massive

The Orleans Factory ruins at Shad Pond.

walls amid trees, brush and briers. There is also another remnant from the past that lingers amid the ruins. It is the ghost of an old man.

Residents and visitors to the site have witnessed this odd specter dressed in nineteenth-century garb hovering about the area of the once-bustling establishment. He appears and vanishes at random without rhyme or reason. A common assumption is that he may have been a factory employee or even the person who was responsible for the final fire in 1884. There is a look of sadness in his eyes, as if still mourning the fate of the former structure.

Feelings of uneasiness and panic as well as unfriendly vibes are reported by those who roam about the ruins. Some people have actually seen the factory as it was in its heyday, on fire, with the ghosts of workers jumping out windows.

Take Route 44 into Rehoboth, turn onto Elm Street and bear right at the fork to Lincoln Street. Take a left onto County Street, which will turn into Providence Street. Bear left onto Reed Street, and the pond and ruins will be on your left. The factory ruins are on Reed Road next to Shad Pond.

Hornbine School

A short trip down Hornbine Road at the intersection of Reed Street brings you to the little old Hornbine schoolhouse. The school was built in 1845 and housed students up to grade nine. It was originally called the Cole Brook School. Its name changed to Hornbine in 1882. Children learned the essentials of education there for almost one hundred years before the school closed its doors in 1937. The building was sold, and the original desks were scrapped for the metal during World War II. The little schoolhouse sat abandoned and fell into ruin, until 1968, when the Hornbine School Association Inc. purchased it and performed renovations in order to hold public tours. The school was added to the National Register of Historic Places in 1983.

The desks in the school at present, though period antiques, are from various parts of the country. The historic building is reminiscent of the typical one-room schools that dotted the nineteenth-century New England landscape. Many examples of these little edifices still exist along the region's back roads. Some are well preserved, and others are mere skeletons of a bygone era. Some, though long abandoned, still hold the ghosts of the past within their walls, and the Hornbine School is one of those where, although the learning may have ceased in the mortal world, lessons continue on the other side of the veil.

The Hornbine School, where class is eternally in session.

Neighbors claim to hear voices and other noises as if the school is in session, yet the building is empty and locked. The ghostly pealing of the school bell is sometimes heard, calling the long-buried pupils to their studies. The bell sat on the teacher's desk, and every morning at nine o'clock, it would be rung to signal the start of class. A few people have attested to hearing voices from the school and, upon investigation, actually seeing the wraiths of a teacher and students dressed in nineteenth-century clothing within the locked building. There is a report of someone knocking on the window, thinking he was witnessing a reenactment. The teacher started walking toward the window with an agitated look on her face before vanishing along with the rest of the figures in the room.

The ghostly class has been witnessed by several people who state that the ghosts carry on the same routine over and over, as if they are not aware they are dead or they are part of a residual haunting that appears at random.

The Hornbine School in Rehoboth is open on the second and fourth Sundays between June and September from two to four o'clock in the afternoon for interested visitors to tour and talk with an association member who can answer their questions. There is no admission charge.

The schoolhouse is located at the corner of Baker Street and Hornbine Road. Follow directions to Shad Pond but stay on Providence Street. Bear left onto Pleasant Street, then take a quick right onto Martin Street. Follow Martin Street across Route 118, then bear right onto Spring Street. Bear left onto Hornbine Road. The school is just ahead on the left. If you are coming from Route 44, bear south on Route 118, then take a right onto Martin Street and follow the above directions.

Palmer River Churchyard Cemetery

A short distance down the road from Shad Pond Factory is the Palmer River Churchyard Cemetery. The cemetery is reportedly haunted by a little boy in nineteenth-century dress. Witnesses claim to have heard the crying of a child within the cemetery. There are Revolutionary War graves in the cemetery where misty figures have been seen walking in the old lanes between the stones. One report is of a grayish-black figure that wanders around the tombstones, and the other is of giant orbs floating above the decrepit monuments. Some believe there are malevolent entities residing in the burial ground. Researchers of the paranormal have gathered voices and noises on recorders suggesting that all are not resting peacefully in this burial ground.

Follow directions to Shad Pond but stay on Providence Street. The cemetery is on the left and clearly marked with a plaque.

The historic and haunted Palmer River Churchyard Cemetery.

A Few More Rehoboth Stories

In 1968, five people witnessed a ball of light floating among the trees in Rehoboth. When they shouted at it, the ball expanded and swiftly moved toward them, forcing them to run from the entity. In another case, a Rehoboth man glanced out into his snow-covered field and saw what looked like a tree burning in the distance. On investigation, he found that no tree had burned and there were no ashes as evidence and no signs in the snow that anyone may have been in the area where he saw the mysterious light.

A Rehoboth resident walking by an old, abandoned barn was interrupted from his stroll one night by a strange screeching noise. As he peered into one of the busted-out windows, he saw a small black figure on the wall staring back at him. The apparition slowly turned into a thick mist and moved through the air toward the person, who turned and fled in fear. On returning to the scene, he heard the same screeching noises but did not venture over for a second look.

Simeon Martin is buried in Burial Place Hill Historical Cemetery No. 33 at the corner of Providence and Peckham Streets. Simeon was born on October 20, 1754, and died on September 3, 1819. He was a successful Rhode Island merchant. When the Revolutionary War broke out, he came to call for the Lexington Alarm and the Siege of Boston. He became lieutenant governor of Rhode Island in 1810 and served for seven years, never reaching the position of governor. When he died in 1819, he was buried under a table stone with a massive epitaph—407 words, the most on any gravestone in the United States and perhaps the world. The tablet is weather worn, but a plaque sits next to the grave with a transcription for one to read if they so desire. It must have been quite a chore for the stone carver.

Creatures of the Bridgewater Triangle

Residents of Southeastern Massachusetts have long been plagued by strange phenomena that have mystified scientists, archaeologists, cryptozoologists, historians and researchers of the paranormal. One of the most famous—if not *the* most famous—areas along US Route 44 lies in what is known as the Bridgewater Triangle. The triangle is a two-hundred-square-mile parcel of land that harbors mythical creatures, ghostly lights, phantoms and even UFOs. The triangle first got its name in the 1970s when researcher Loren Coleman carried out paranormal investigations in the area. Following extensive research and studies, he mapped out a triangle where the strange phenomena seemed intensely active. Christopher Balzano, a paranormal investigator and author, compiled astounding data on the area. He used this data to write several books, including *Ghosts of the Bridgewater Triangle.*

The corners of the triangle are defined by the towns of Abington, Freetown and Rehoboth. Within the triangle are the towns of Taunton, Brockton, Raynham, Bridgewater, Marshfield, Norton, Easton, North Middleboro, Segragonset, Dighton, North Dighton, Berkeley and Myricks. Within the triangle lies the Hockomock Swamp, where much of the activity is focused. Accounts of strange creatures in the triangle abound. Here are some that have stunned researchers and scientists alike.

There have been many reports in the area and near the swamp that sits off Route 138 of a phantom described as a small person with gangling arms that look as if they are broken and swinging freely as it moves. Some have seen the creature on the wall near the roadside, and others reported it coming out of the woods almost into the path of their automobile before running back into the brush on the side of the road. Could this creature be an elemental or perhaps another incarnation of the famous Dover Demon?

In 1988, two boys followed a pair of giant three-toed footprints into the swamp. To their horror, they came upon a massive birdlike creature that neither had ever witnessed the likes of in their life. The winged monster caught a glimpse of the two boys and took off straight into the air. The frightened youths ran for their lives, later ranting their story to police and neighbors. It was concluded that the two youths had seen a great blue heron, a very large bird native to the New England area. The children swore the creature they saw was much larger than any heron, more the size of a tall man with half-human features. The story was almost laughable until someone remembered another similar sighting. This one was by a well-known Norton police sergeant named Thomas Downy.

In 1971, as Sergeant Downy was driving home along Winter Street in Marshfield, he came upon a giant creature standing at the edge of the swamp. According to the officer, it resembled a bird but stood over six feet tall. The creature moved toward the car, then flew straight up away from the vehicle. It had a wingspan of about eight to twelve feet. When other officers arrived at the scene, a few large three-toed footprints were all that was found as evidence of such a creature. Oddly enough, the sighting was at a place called Bird Hill, where the Indigenous people frequently spoke of a legendary Thunderbird. Their ancestors claimed the great bird lived in the swamp—and, to this day, it apparently still does.

Thunderbirds are not solely responsible for the cryptid sightings within Bridgewater Triangle. A more famous and often talked about "monster" is reported to roam the area. It is the creature affectionately known as Bigfoot, Yeti or Sasquatch. In 1970, residents reported seeing a hairy seven-foot monster running through their yards, sometimes on all four legs. Local and state police conducted a lengthy search for a giant bear, yet no such animal was ever spotted or captured.

On April 8, 1970, two officers were parked in a police cruiser near the swamp. Suddenly, the car's rear end lifted into the air and then dropped with a loud bang. The officers quickly spun the car around and trained their spotlight on something hairy resembling a bear as it ran on two legs behind a house. A thorough search of the area commenced, but no bear or other creature was ever found.

A hunter once shot at a large animal in the woods that ran off and gave a half-human, half-animal cry. Later, the hunter found brown hair and blood on some leaves along the path the creature fled down. A woman in West Bridgewater heard a noise one night in her yard. She looked out her window and saw a large bipedal creature eating a pumpkin in her garden. The hairy animal looked at her through the window with reddish-orange eyes and then, with a grunt, took off with the pumpkin into the woods.

A triangle resident, Joseph M. De Andrade, spent decades collecting reports of the creature. The average lifespan of a wild bear is five to seven years. Fifteen years would be improbable, and thirty years in the wild is impossible. So what is it out there, roaming along the outskirts of the human population?

Andrade witnessed a Bigfoot in 1978. He spied a huge, strange-looking creature walking down a hill about two hundred feet in front of him. Andrade described it as over six feet tall, brown and hairy. He could not see its face, as it was walking away from him. Since then, he has recorded many accounts of the "Bridgewater Bigfoot." Andrade would later go on video describing his account and showing a representation of what he saw. It was not the first time he had encountered the creature. Once, while collecting firewood during a camping trip, he heard a thunderous growl he would later describe as sounding like "something from hell." His campmates also heard the roar. In all their years of camping in those woods, they had never heard any such sound. Whatever it was, it was very close and gave them the impression it did not want them there.

Three other campers pitched a tent in the woods near the swamp. Shortly after they set up camp, something threw a large log at them, causing the party to vacate the premises. The following day, they returned to fetch their gear and tried to lift the log. All three had great difficulty hoisting it off the ground. Whatever it was possessed immense strength to be able to catapult the massive piece of wood into the campsite.

John Baker of West Bridgeport, Massachusetts, witnessed the "Bigfoot" monster in the early 1980s. While hunting in the swamp, he had the feeling that someone or something was following him. He turned and saw a large, hairy beast standing in the brush along the water's edge only a few yards from him. The "thing" was tall and covered with hair and smelled very badly. It turned and ran off into the woods. Baker has since searched for the creature but has never come across it since that fateful day.

Reports of a giant dog once circulated within the swamp region. The creature was alleged to be the size of a pony and had even attacked a few people. For several weeks, the hound from hell terrorized the area, keeping one step ahead of search parties. One police officer actually came upon the monster and fired a shot at it. Whether or not the bullet hit the animal is not known. The animal ran off into the swamp, never to be seen again.

One of New England's oldest and most amazing legends about strange creatures is that of a small being called a Pukwudgie. *Pukwudgie* or *Puk-Wudjie* roughly translates into English as "wild man of the woods" or "little wild man of the woods that vanishes." These human-like little demons are deeply steeped in Wampanoag folklore and are considered the oldest and most dangerous mythical creatures in North America. Author, educator and historian Christopher Balzano hit it right on the nose when he stated, in his book *Dark Woods,*

> *Large monsters are intimidating, but cannot fit under the bed, or in the closet, or in the corner of the room just beyond where the illumination hits. Small monsters can hide, sneak into thin cracks and slip out of sight.*

The Pukwudgie is known to do just that and more. The creature is described as two to three feet tall, covered in hair from head to toe, resembling a troll. Pukwudgies have the power to appear and disappear at will, lure people to their deaths, shape-shift into various animals, shoot poison arrows and instantly create fire. Anyone who gets on the wrong side of a Pukwudgie is bound to meet with horrible circumstances.

According to Wampanoag legend, the Pukwudgies were friendly and helpful to humans until the tribe, thinking they were a nuisance, had the giant Maushop rid the area of them. Some survived and remained in Bridgewater Triangle area, wreaking havoc on those who crossed their path.

Stories of these evil fairies go as far back as the written word but, for some reason, were not well received until the early twentieth century, when Elizabeth Reynard published *The Narrow Land: Folk Chronicles of Old Cape Cod*. Within this book are several Wampanoag legends, including that of the Pukwudgie. More recent accounts have flooded the pages of books; daily, weekly and monthly publications; and the internet.

Pukwudgies also use the souls of the dead to lure victims to their demise. One person followed a ball of light into the woods only to spot one of the diminutive demons trying to lure him in further. A few nights later, in the same area, the same creature stalked this person while he sat in his auto.

One of the more interesting warnings against the evil demons in recent times was the placement of a sign along Slab Bridge Road near the Freetown State Forest reading, "PUKWUDGIE XING."

If you decide to look for Pukwudgies, be careful and do not annoy them. Many people in the area who have encountered the mystical creatures will tell you that some things are often better left alone.

Not all phenomena in the triangle are restricted to the ground. On May 10, 1760, at about ten o'clock in the morning, two residents observed a fiery sphere of light moving across the sky. Not much else is recorded on the incident. On October 31, 1908, two undertakers were driving a carriage from West Bridgewater when they witnessed an object in the sky. They described the object as looking like an unusually bright lantern about two and a half feet in diameter, illuminating a larger object resembling a balloon bag. For nearly forty minutes, the witnesses watched the object move in a straight line, then turn abruptly and move again in a straight line. All balloon ascensions in the area were accounted for, though none of the movements made by the UFO was anything a balloon was capable of. The undertakers wrote that the object, unlike an air balloon, moved in small circles—up, down and perpendicular—at will. The object also made no noise as it moved with such agility in the sky. On that date in 1908, there were no airplanes in the sky such as we see today. Whatever it was truly remains an enigma.

CHAPTER 2
RHODE ISLAND

EAST PROVIDENCE TO GLOCESTER, 26.3 MILES (42.3 KM)
Looff Carousel, East Providence

While you are roaming the East Providence area, you may want to take a ride on a haunted carousel. Charles I.D. Looff, one of the first and foremost designers of carousels, built the historical gem that sits in East Providence in 1895. It became his flagship work of art for prospective buyers, being the largest and most elaborate carousel he had created to date. The carousel features sixty-one hand-carved horses, a camel, four chariots, beveled mirrors, faceted jewels, sandwich glass and a German band organ built by A. Ruth & Sohn that brings present-day riders back to the past. Strangely, though, the past seems to keep coming back to the present.

From 1886 to 1977, people worldwide flocked to enjoy the rides, entertainment, sea air and shore dinners for which Rhode Island became famous. The carousel was part of an amusement facility called Crescent Park. The famous Alhambra Ballroom burned on September 2, 1969, causing a significant blow to the already declining park. Over time, changes in ownership, equipment failures and fires led to the park's closing in 1977. In 1979, the rides and other accouterments were auctioned off. All that remained was the Looff carousel. When the carousel was threatened with demolition, a group of residents got together and saved it. Apparently, it

The horses of the Looff Carousel await riders.

was a great move, as the Charles Looff Carousel was not only placed on the National Register of Historic Places in 1976 but also recognized by the State of Rhode Island as a "State Jewel of American Folk Art" and by the National Park Service as a National Historic Landmark in 1987.

The Looff Carousel boasts over 11.6 million riders and counting since it opened over a century ago. As of this writing, tickets are two dollars or twenty for thirty dollars, and they never expire. Children under age three ride for free. So many people have left the one-hundred-foot circumference building feeling the awe of the past—but some have never dismounted the beautiful yet foreboding horses.

Employees often experience the music from the organ turning on by itself when they enter the building. The lights also begin to flicker as though the carousel is about to start its revolutions around the building, hosting ghostly riders that still revel in the spirit of the now historic carousel.

People who live around the carousel witnessed paranormal phenomena as the land where the park once sat became a housing development. They occasionally hear the music and see the carousel light up as the horses ready themselves for another ride. A woman in a hoop skirt has been seen looking out over the water. No one knows who she is, but she evidently was attracted to the place in life as she haunts it after death.

The Looff Carousel refuses to remain silent.

The summer is the best time to visit the carousel for a ride into the past. The bike path that passes by the carousel was once a railway. Though long gone, the sound of a train is still heard, and flashing lights are seen on the old tracks.

The carousel is located at 700 Bullocks Point Avenue, Riverside, Rhode Island.

UFO Encounter, East Providence

On October 19, 2018, one, maybe two, multicolored UFOs were witnessed at about two o'clock in the morning from a supermarket parking lot on Taunton Avenue (Route 44) in East Providence, Rhode Island. The object was estimated at about five thousand feet, moving up and down and side to side as if searching for something. The lights dimmed and brightened as the strange vessel moved about before shooting off into space.

Providence

Providence is the capital city of Rhode Island. It was initially settled in 1636 when Roger Williams and his band of dissenters were banished from the Plymouth Bay Colony for their religious beliefs. They eventually settled on what is now College Hill, led there by divine "providence," and began a flourishing colony. Today, Providence is a Renaissance city with many diverse and eclectic places to visit. From College Hill to Federal Hill, Providence's history reflects the cultures that have made it a destination. And, of course, it is not without plenty of haunted places.

One interesting tidbit as Route 44 leaves the city: near LaSalle Academy sits a small brown house, once the home of Mary Ann Angell, one of the many wives of Mormon leader Brigham Young.

Providence City Hall

Providence City Hall sits on the southwest end of Kennedy Plaza at 25 Dorrance Street. The building, constructed between 1875 and 1878 and designed by Samuel J.F. Thayer, is a Second Empire design. In 1975, the building was listed on the National Register of Historic Places. The building

Providence City Hall is famous for its ghosts. *Author's collection.*

has some resident ghosts that have made enough noise for employees to have the place featured on a popular television show in 2012.

Some phenomena include chairs moving, breezes stirring as if someone is quickly passing by, whispers, people being touched, doors slamming and drawers opening on their own. Other strange occurrences reported are names being called out by phantom voices, shadow figures moving across rooms, a spectral rider on the elevator and an instance where an employee clearly heard someone say to her, "Not today."

There is speculation that at least one of the ghosts may be that of a former mayor, Thomas Doyle, who was also, at one point, the city sergeant. Although some of the phenomena may be explained rationally, the rest are still what is easily termed paranormal in nature.

Roger Williams Tree

If there is one Providence story that takes the "strange" award, this is it. Roger Williams and his band came to Providence after being ousted from the Plymouth colony for their religious dissension. They settled on what is now the East Side, trading with the local Indigenous tribes. As time passed, Williams built a trading post in South County where he could barter with locals.

Roger Williams statue in Prospect Terrace, where the founder of the state's mortal remains are now buried.

Williams and his wife, Mary, had six children. He died in 1683 at the age of eighty and was buried in his backyard. In 1860, it was decided that the state of Rhode Island's founder should be interred in a more suitable place of recognition, so his body was exhumed.

Among the remains were nails, teeth and bone fragments, all expected to be what was left—but nature had intervened in a macabre way. An apple tree had grown on the spot where Williams was buried. The roots had entered the coffin, penetrated Williams's head and then entered the chest cavity before splitting at the legs and turning upward at the feet.

The nails, teeth and bone fragments were reburied in the Old North Burial Ground, where they lay until 1936, when they were exhumed once again and buried under the statue of Williams at Prospect Terrace. The statue at 188 Pratt Street sits across from the lot that Williams's house once graced and can almost be spied from Route 44. The root is on display in the Brown Museum Carriage House inside a coffin-shaped frame protected by a wire screen.

An apple tree with which many people likely sated their hunger ended up consuming the founder of Rhode Island. Some people may unknowingly have Roger Williams's blood in their family roots.

The root is the closest likeness we have of the founder of Rhode Island, as he never sat for a portrait.

Benefit Street

Benefit Street was originally called Back Street by the first settlers, as it cut along the back of Providence. As prominent people took to this new city, they chose the hill overlooking the Providence River, where the less affluent could look up at the stately houses with awe and envy.

By 1770, it became necessary to widen the road and straighten its winding curves for ease of travel. As this would benefit travelers along the road, it was renamed Benefit Street. Many of the homes remain much as they did back in the eighteenth and nineteenth centuries when they were constructed. Due to the lack of a formal burial ground, the townsfolk initially interred their loved ones in their own yards. When renovations took place on Back Street, many of these deceased were exhumed and removed to the newly built North Burial Ground. Some are convinced that this mass exhumation became a catalyst for the ghostly activity that now plagues the area. Although this may be so, several other famous people have lent their ethereal services to making Benefit Street the most haunted neighborhood in Providence.

Edgar Allan Poe was no stranger to Providence. His last love, Sarah Helen Whitman, resided at what is now 88 Benefit Street. Many have seen a man resembling the great writer cloaked in black, adorned with a top hat and carrying a walking stick (fashionable for Poe's time), meandering along the street late at night. Poe was to marry Whitman, but the nuptials were called off when he showed up at her door just before the wedding incoherent and drunk. His ghost is seen approaching the doorstep of Whitman's former home, then vanishing. Poe and Whitman also haunt the Athenaeum, where they frequently visited. Poe is also said to haunt the cemetery near the Whitman Home. This small churchyard is where he originally proposed to Whitman.

Poe attended the University of Virginia for a semester and became a cadet at West Point after enlisting in the army in 1827. He reached the rank of sergeant major, the highest noncommissioned rank one could receive. Unfortunately, his writing beckoned. He began composing poems while writing for several journals and periodicals. In 1836, he married his thirteen-year-old cousin, Virginia Clemm, but tragically, she died of tuberculosis on January 30, 1847. Poe had been drinking heavily due to the stress of her illness.

Sarah Helen Whitman house on Providence's East Side, where Edgar Allan Poe's ghost is sometimes seen.

The Providence Athenaeum, where Edgar Allan Poe wooed Sarah Helen Whitman.

Shortly after Virginia's death, he started courting Sarah Helen Whitman of Providence, Rhode Island, whom he had met in July 1845. Whitman, a poet and spiritualist, was an ardent fan of Poe's work. They exchanged letters for a period until he proposed, and she accepted on the condition he remain sober until the day of the wedding. This he promised, but the vow lasted only a few days. He began drinking again and even attempted to kill himself. After speaking at a lecture in Providence, he met up with a few of his nefarious friends, and they went out for a drink. Poe had obviously had a few drinks too many when he showed up at her door inebriated. That was all she could stand. Whitman officially broke off her engagement with the author on December 23, 1848. Poe was also accused of pursuing a woman named Nancy Richmond and his childhood sweetheart Sarah Elmira Royster by Whitman's mother. In a letter to Whitman addressed "Dear Madam," Poe noted that he blamed her mother for their failed relationship.

The Providence Athenaeum was one of the couple's favorite haunts in life. It appears to be Poe's in death, as well. An extraordinary event was recorded in the 1980s and has replayed many times since. A passerby saw a disheveled man sleeping on the stairs of the Athenaeum late one night. His rough, drunken appearance gave rise to the thought that he was homeless and could use some aid. The passerby approached the man, offering to help him in any way he could. The vagabond awoke, and with a dreary, solemn look, he replied, "I was dreaming of the conqueror worm. I thank you for waking me."

Satisfied that the man did not need assistance, the passerby continued on, but after a few feet, he turned one more time and glanced back at the character on the stairs. At that instant, the figure became misty and slowly dissipated before his eyes. As the lights from the street shone on the face of the poor soul, the passerby saw it was none other than the countenance of Poe himself.

Poe frequently stayed at the Mansion House Hotel during his visits to Providence. A former tenant found an old slipper belonging to a woman in his bedroom closet. When no one came forward to claim the lost item, he discarded it, and from that night until he vacated the property, he was roused from his sleep by the distinct sound of a Victorian skirt rustling in his room, as if someone was in search of something. Could it have been the ghost of Sara Helen Whitman trying to reclaim lost property?

Rhode Island School of Design

Rhode Island School of Design (RISD) was founded in 1877 by a small group of women led by Helen Adelia Rowe Metcalf, who sought to establish a school of art and design. The original plan was to help support the growing textile and jewelry industry that Rhode Island was already famous for. Courses included freehand drawing, mechanical drawing and design and painting.

Since its inception, RISD has stood out as not only one of the first independent colleges of art and design in America but also a continuing legacy for the students who have moved forward in their chosen field. The years have also nourished a few who may have returned in the afterlife.

Rhode Island School of Design has buildings lacing the area, and many of them are reported to be haunted. Many stories have circulated over the years pertaining to the ghosts on College Hill, just off Route 44. Some allege that several of the buildings were built on the family graveyards that were prominent in the early days of the hill area.

Barstow House is said to hold demonic entities that cause extreme cold and depression. If one is up late at night, the vast mirrors will reflect the spirits reported to dwell within the house. The Dexter House at 187 Benefit Street was once a morgue, so it may be no surprise that the spirits of those whose bodies were brought there still roam the halls of the building. The Dunnell House, located close by on Angell Street, has a ghost or two in the basement. The face of an old woman has been seen peering out a second-story window by people passing the home.

Homer Hall and Farnum Hall also are home to some former tenants—in Homer Hall, a man and woman who like to break personal items and turn the water faucets on. Two child ghosts who love to play in the basement and a woman who is seen on the second floor occupy the Pardon Miller House on Angell Street, also close to Benefit Street. Perhaps she is in eternal pursuit of the two children—they may have been hers in life but are now separated by physical walls in death.

The Nightingale-Brown House is home to perhaps the most interesting of the college haunts. This building, located at 357 Benefit Street, is owned by Brown University and houses the John Nicholas Brown Center for Public Humanities and Cultural Heritage. It is also the permanent home of one of its previous owners. The Nightingale family sold the house to Nicholas Brown in 1814. The Brown family resided in the home from that time until 1985, when they gifted it to the school.

One evening, two custodians were tidying up the building. The senior custodian was upstairs while the newly hired hand was cleaning the first floor. As the newer custodian performed his nightly task, he had the uncanny feeling that the eyes of one of the portraits were following his every move. Having become a bit unnerved but happy to finish his job, the man exited the room, shutting off the lights behind him. In an instant, a loud voice erupted from the chamber, "Do not turn the lights off!"

The frightened man raced up the stairs to find his coworker where he frantically recounted what had just transpired. On hearing the story, the senior custodian calmly stated, "Yeah, we all know about the portrait and that it speaks. Just don't listen to it, and by all means, never turn the lights off in that room."

One of the eeriest haunts on Benefit Street is the phantom carriage. One evening, a college professor decided to take a late-night walk along the historic street. As he strolled along the moonlit way, something caught his eye. He turned and saw a horse-drawn carriage moving quietly down the empty street. The wheels turned, and the horse's hooves pounded the pavement; however, no sound whatsoever could be heard. The carriage moved silently down the lane and out of sight.

According to legend, an eight-year-old boy named George Kelly was killed when the carriage he was riding in ran into a pothole, ejecting him from the vehicle and running over him. On the first chilly fall evening of the year, the carriage silently makes its way down Benefit Street, vanishing in the night mist.

Over the years, many have witnessed the spectral horse and carriage as they parade without a sound down haunted Benefit Street.

Howard Phillips Lovecraft Haunts

"I am Providence" is the epitaph on the small stone adorning the grave of one of the greatest horror and science fiction writers. It was put there in 1968 by a group of Lovecraft's devoted fans based on what the writer once said: "I am Providence and Providence is me."

Unlike Poe, Lovecraft has never left the city he was born in—at least not in spirit. There are several places where he lived and haunted in life. One place in particular is of special interest because it was where, during his early life, he could hide out and dream of a universe bigger than anyone else could imagine, a universe beyond the stars. Howard Phillips Lovecraft has the Ladd Observatory to hang around in, just as he did when he walked this earth in a mortal frame. Although Lovecraft, like Poe, was a regular at the Athenaeum, he seems to prefer the solitude of the observatory to make his ghostly rounds.

The Ladd Observatory opened in 1891 with a generous donation from Governor Herbert Ladd. Winslow Upton, a Brown University professor of astronomy, became its first director. Upton was fond of young Lovecraft and his passion for the stars. He even gave Lovecraft a key to the observatory so the budding young astronomer could come and go as he pleased. Lovecraft later wrote, in a November 16, 1916 letter to Reinhardt Kleiner,

> *The late Prof. Upton of Brown, a friend of the family, gave me the freedom of the college observatory, & I came & went there at will on my bicycle. Ladd Observatory tops a considerable eminence about a mile from the house. I used to walk up Doyle Avenue with my wheel, but when returning would have a glorious coast down it....I suppose I pestered the people at the observatory half to death, but they were very kind about it.*

Upton may be long gone, but Lovecraft seems to come and go as he pleases. His apparition has been witnessed on the grounds of the building, and neighbors have seen him peering out the windows of the historic

The Ladd Observatory, where Howard Phillips Lovecraft spent much of his youth.

structure. Perhaps his stories are not as far-fetched as some may think. It seems Howard Phillips Lovecraft still clings to the one place in life that gave him much comfort and inspiration.

The observatory is located at 210 Doyle Avenue on the corner of Hope Street. A staircase and elevator lead to a balcony, providing stargazing through several portable telescopes, including the main twelve-inch refractor. One can examine vintage equipment from the observatory's early days on the first floor. The observatory is open to the public on clear Tuesday evenings.

One particular item to note for those who may want an extra dose of Lovecraftian fare: each year, Keith and Carl Johnson, second cousins twice removed from H.P., host a special tribute to the legendary writer. The event takes place at the observatory around the calendar date of his death. After the tribute, a tour of his grave at Swan Point Cemetery and a few other Lovecraft sites round out a perfect Lovecraftian day. If you should happen to get a glimpse of the writer's ghost, then the day would be nothing less than absolutely perfect.

Brown University

Brown University is one of the country's leading institutions of higher education. Like many other facilities of its kind, it is rife with ghosts and strange sensations that overcome those who wander into a certain area of the campus. One particular area is University Hall, built in 1770 and the oldest building on campus. The hall served as living quarters and classrooms during the first years of the school. It later served as a barracks and hospital for the Continental army starting in 1776, when the British landed in Newport. As recounted in *Early History of Brown University, Including the Life, Times, and Correspondence of President Manning, 1756–1791*, Brown's first president, Reverend James Hilton Manning, wrote,

> *The College edifice was first taken in December, 1776, for the use of barracks and a hospital for the American troops, and retained for that use until the Fall before the arrival of his most Christian Majesty's fleets and armies in this State....By our direction, the President resumed the course of education in said College, and took possession of the edifice on May 10, 1780; and continued so to occupy it until the authority of this State, in a short time after, granted it to the French army as a hospital, who continued to hold and use it for said purpose until the last week, when the Commissary of War of the French army delivered it up, with the keys, to his Honor the Deputy Governor; they having previously permitted the officers of the French ships in this State to place their sick in it, who still continue there... and the other, a horse stable, built from the east projection to the north end, by which the house is greatly weakened.*

The mention of the stable is significant in the haunting of the building. People have witnessed a man leading a horse through a wall in the former stable area as if there is still a door there. The ghost of a Revolutionary War soldier is often seen on the second floor. People passing by have seen him peering out one of the windows, perhaps looking out for the enemy. Footsteps are heard in areas of the building when there is no one else there to cause such a noise. Dire cries are heard echoing through the rooms and halls. It seems there are still some from long past trapped within the confines of University Hall. Take College Hill off Route 44, and you will see the great edifice. A bit of advice: a lot of students would never dare set foot in the building. Perhaps they are just superstitious; perhaps more…

University Hall at Brown University has ghosts from all eras.

While you are in the area, you may want to visit the John Hay Library and peruse its H. Adrian Smith Collection of Conjuring and Magicana. It is the finest collection of its kind, featuring three thousand books and items related to witchcraft, astrology, alchemy and other occult sciences and practices. It's no wonder there are so many witches roaming and residing on the East Side of Providence.

UFOs over Providence

On August 12, 1965, an unnamed astronomy enthusiast and a few friends were perusing the night sky over Providence, Rhode Island, with a 120-power telescope when, at about eleven o'clock, one of them saw two objects with bright yellow lights moving across the sky toward the west-northwest. They were estimated to be flying at about seven thousand feet. The objects made no sound as they moved about before vanishing into the night sky.

The amateur astronomer contacted the Air National Guard; Quonset Point Naval Station in Kingstown, Rhode Island; and the airport. None of them reported having any flights in the air at the time of the sighting.

In June 2000, a pilot flying at eight thousand feet spotted what he thought at first was a large bird in his flight path. As the figure grew closer, he saw it was actually an egg-shaped object standing upright with three distinct points on both ends. The craft passed very close to the wing of his plane, causing the pilot to contact air traffic control. They radioed back, stating that there was a craft, unknown and unidentified, following about one mile behind his.

The Old Swamp on Route 44, Greenville

Before Route 44 was built many years ago, horses and buggies ruled the small two-lane road once known as the Powder Mill Turnpike. Across from where the Walgreens and A&W sit on Route 44 in Greenville, a village in the town of Smithfield, was a swamp. The swamp has long since disappeared due to progress, but it was vast and deep at one time.

According to the story, a horse and buggy were traveling down the road when something suddenly spooked the horse, causing it to buck and run off the road, taking the buggy and rider with it into the swamp. They all sank into the muck, never to be seen again—until improvements were made to the area. That is when a gruesome discovery was made. While digging in the swamp, workers discovered the remains of a buggy, horse and driver buried deep in the mire. The mystery of their sudden disappearance many years prior was solved, but to this day, it is said the area is haunted by the ghost horse and buggy.

Greenville Public Library

Libraries are one of America's most incredible free resources. There is so much to see and do at a library, from presentations to activities and a vast array of items you can borrow. Some libraries now offer ghost-hunting kits one can borrow for a few days.

The old and new books are always a treasure to sort through. An afternoon can fly by while visiting a library. In some cases, there are those who have remained much longer.

The Greenville Public Library is home to a few ghosts who love roaming the rooms and playing with the books on the shelves. The old library once stood at the town common but soon became too small to accommodate the number of books that were being donated.

The Jenckes family donated land to the town for a new library, razing several small outbuildings and moving their home to a location beside the new building. When the library was built, a beautiful stone building was also donated for storage and conferences. The town eventually tore the building down to expand the parking lot. This may have set off old Mrs. Jenckes, who not only donated the land in 1938 but also served as the library's longtime trustee. The present library was commissioned on October 18, 1955.

The library was built on the original Jenckes house foundation but was later expanded to meet the library's growing inventory. The original basement is still part of the lower level of the library and seems to be the most haunted place in the building. Many patrons have reported the uncanny feeling of being watched by some unseen presence while on the library's lower floor.

A grand piano sits downstairs in one of the rooms. People have heard the sound of the piano when no one was there. A visitor studying in the basement once heard the piano start playing. When they entered the room, the music abruptly stopped, and the room was completely empty. There was absolutely no way anyone could have left the room unseen, as the door was the only entrance and egress. These occurrences take place at random hours throughout the day and night.

Much of the staff credits Mrs. Jenckes for the ghostly deeds. Some nights, staff will turn the lights off in the basement and by the time they are back on the first floor, all the lights are turned on again. Books fall from the shelves in front of witnesses as if an unseen hand is pulling them from their resting place.

Two staff members once witnessed a whole row of books slide from the shelf onto the floor like someone had taken their arm and pushed the books from behind. Library employees occasionally hear the thud of a book falling from the shelves as if someone or something dropped it. Some claim it might not be Mrs. Jenckes making all the mischief. Several staff members believe the spirit of the first librarian, Orra Angell, may be to blame for some of the occurrences. Angell was the village librarian in 1882 when the library was located down the street across from the common.

Whether it may be Mrs. Angell or Mrs. Jenckes, or both, does not make much difference, as many of the library workers and a few patrons will not venture down into the lower chambers alone for fear of confronting a restless spirit of the Greenville Public Library.

The library is located at 573 Putnam Pike, just before the Greenville Common.

The Resolved Waterman Tavern, Greenville

The Resolved Waterman Tavern sits in the center of Greenville, Rhode Island, as a historic landmark and tribute to the bygone era of stagecoach travel and tavern life. The building one sees today is but a fraction the original tavern. The inn was originally *T*-shaped, with the eastern and western walls connected by a courtyard. A large dining hall occupied the first floor, with a dance hall directly above. This building is the earliest tavern on record in Smithfield. Resolved Waterman (1703–1746) erected the tavern in 1733 at the crossroads in Greenville just after the completion of the Providence/ Putnam Turnpike (Route 44).

The tavern quickly became a popular stop along the busy pike; travelers and locals mingled, sharing stories and the latest news over drinks and victuals, or danced the night away at hoedowns. In fact, Waterman's tavern became such a favored rest stop that it rarely stayed vacant. During the American Revolution, the tavern was a meeting place for patriots. Daniel Mowry and Peleg Arnold, both members of the Continental Congress, held meetings there.

One evening, a traveling peddler came to lodge at the inn. Unfortunately, all the rooms were full, but Waterman, being a kind man, offered him lodging in the root cellar. The traveler ate and drank his fill until he was ready to retire for the night. He stumbled down the narrow stairs to the makeshift accommodations to sleep off his excessive indulgence. That was the last anyone ever saw of him—in the flesh, anyway.

The following day, the peddler's bag of wares and belongings was found beside his bed, but he had simply vanished without a trace. It was soon agreed that he might have risen in the dead of night and, stumbling around in the dark, fallen into the well in the basement. Resolved Waterman, fearing this and the fact that it could happen again, sealed the well and dug another in a safer, more secluded spot. Within a few weeks of this incident, guests began seeing the ghost of the peddler roaming around the building. Regulars swore it was the shade of the peddler they all shared drinks with on that fateful night he mysteriously disappeared.

Another story concerns an anonymous traveler who stopped in one night for some refreshment and rest. After a few drinks, the man opened his pack and pulled out a pet rattlesnake. Claiming the snake could do tricks, he released it in the tavern. Whether the snake performed any tricks or not was not recorded. The snake slithered up the chimney of the taproom fireplace, and when the man went to get him, he was bitten with a deadly dose of

Old Route 44 stage line. *Author's collection.*

The restored and haunted Resolved Waterman Tavern.

venom. Not knowing who he was or where he was from, the locals buried the man in an unmarked grave on the outskirts of the village. Perhaps his ghost has returned to find peace or even his beloved snake.

Another boarder once roomed in the cellar for the evening but got the fright of his life when a pair of scissors seemed to take on wings and flew past his head. Needless to say, the guest took his belongings and cut out of the building in a hurry.

As time passed, so did the owners of the haunted inn. In 1822, the building became the home of the Smithfield Exchange Bank. The bank folded in 1856, but the massive safe stayed on the first floor of the building. In 1867, the building was a tavern under the ownership of Albert Mowry. During this time, a large firebox was put in the cellar, where a sixty-gallon copper kettle was used to make rum. In 1936, the front section of the building was razed to allow the expansion of Putnam Pike. The last inhabitant of the house was Bessie Fish. For many years, the building stood vacant and prone to vandals. In 2003, the Smithfield Preservation Society acquired the crumbling building and began renovations. The building is now a museum, complete with an upper meeting hall, the safe on the first floor where banking was done and other important historical artifacts throughout the building.

The ghost of the peddler is still said to haunt the structure as you read this. The home is occasionally open for tours, and those who venture into the building get a glimpse into history. Who knows? You may even get a tour from a man resembling an eighteenth-century peddler.

UFO over Slack's Reservoir, Greenville

Just a few hundred yards off Route 44 in Greenville is Terrace View Drive, a small road that skirts the edge of Slack's Reservoir. In November 1958, a massive glowing object resembling two dinner plates stacked one right side up and the other upside down on top of each other covered most of the sky to the southwest. A glowing yellow-green band separated the two "plates" as they rotated slowly while hovering above the water.

Moments later, five smaller objects met the craft, merging with it. The observer noted that there was no sound at all during the entire duration the ship was present. The beholder of this event would later attest that he may have witnessed an alien mother ship and five smaller scout vessels.

While You Are There: The "Haunted" City, Smithfield

In the northwest corner of Smithfield, buried deep in the woods, lies a ghost town known as Hanton City or "Haunted City." The remains of this lost settlement sit in a wooded area known as Island Woods due to the small hills rising out of the swamps within the overgrowth.

The abandoned town is rich with mystery: Who were its founders? Why did they settle there? What became of them? Theorists and historians speculate about everything from runaway slaves to British army deserters or even plague victims banished to the woods to keep them from infecting the general populace. We do know that the Hantons—an early Yankee version of the names Harrington, Herrindeen, Horndean or Haerndon—were numerous in the three-thousand-acre settlement. The little village stood for a while and was abandoned as fast as it was settled. Most of the people moved to better locations as roads and other improvements due to progress took place. The most logical reasons the people of the haunted city may have vanished from the area were the poor farming conditions and industry growth outside the settlement. Bustling factories

Foundation of a former home in Hanton City. *Photo courtesy of Jim Ignasher.*

provided jobs and a place to live for those who migrated out of the fields and woods to join the modern world. The Hantons, however, stayed with their homesteads well into the latter half of the nineteenth century until they finally died off, leaving the area to memories and the spirits that linger among the ruins.

Many of the remains are still visible along the old roads. Numerous home foundations, wells, corncrib stilts, walls, a portion of the old school/meetinghouse and a few colonial burying grounds—the ruins seem to spring out from behind brush or appear around every corner. Hiking the overgrown roads is quite an experience, as they are among the oldest in the state and still accessible. Although many areas of the land are private property, the Smithfield Land Trust owns a good section of Hanton City.

Within the land trust boundaries sits a large boulder with a natural basin in the center. This is known as the threshing or "thrashing" rock. Both Indigenous peoples and settlers used this basin to winnow their grain or separate the heads of wheat from the stalks. Excavations at some of the sites revealed much about the daily life of those who lived in the haunted city. Researchers used pipe fragments, ox shoes and fragments of dishes and small tools to estimate when the place was inhabited.

The *Observer*, a local weekly publication, offered two articles in May and August 1972 about the place locals called the Rumbly. The articles refer to Hanton City as "a real village that sank into the middle of Cedar Swamp like the lost city of Atlantis."

The main road through the village was given the name Rumbly due to its surface's rough, barely navigable condition. The paper stated: "There are old timers, or were until recently, who still had recollections of the 'ride through the rumbly,' that eerie, ghost-ridden place called Hanton City Road."

On this road once stood a small stone building where the Hanton City folk left rum and gingerbread for those passing through to eat and drink. "They speak of a stone house by the roadside where refreshments were left for weary travelers who could pay or not, as they were able. This food, a jug of rum and some gingerbread, was supposedly set out by the mysterious Hantons."

Several old-timers hunting in the old city recalled instances where their rifles were wrenched from their hands, landing several feet away. People hiking through the old village have also heard children laughing and playing in the perimeters of the house ruins. People hiking the old roads are often overcome by a strange, fearful feeling that someone or something is watching them.

In 2015, cable television show host Charles Gardiner and his crew—Dan Case, Matt McDermott and David Chadronet—toured the abandoned village to see what they could find. The following incident took place at what is known as the Hermit's House. Witnesses attest to having seen a misty apparition floating about near the remains of the home. At one of the foundations, Charles recorded a woman's voice whispering. The fact that no women were present at the time and all were very quiet during the recording session made this piece of evidence quite valuable in the sphere of strange activity reported within Hanton City.

Another area where supernatural phenomenon has been reported is the Brown Cemetery. The small family burying ground has about fifteen burials marked with hand-hewn field stones. A few of the stones are carved with crude inscriptions. One reads "A.B. 1774" and the other "D.B. May 1784."

D.B. was most likely Daniel Brown and A.B. Alice Haernton Brown, daughter of Benjamin Haernton. This location is another place where people hear ethereal voices and see shadows moving out of the corners of their eyes within the small cemetery. It could be paranormal or perhaps just the natural movement of the trees and brush swaying in the wind, playing tricks on them. In Hanton City, anything is possible.

There is also a site on the trail's edge where six upright stones beckon the curious. These were most likely used for a corncrib. The home foundation with stone indents resembling shelves behind the six standing stones is in remarkable condition for its age. Hikers have also recorded EVPs at this site. In 2014, a small group of researchers encountered a voice that permeated the air, not in a loud tone but as if it was right beside the party. The voice clearly said, "Inside the barn." They all froze at first, wondering where it came from, as the group was deep in the woods with no one else around. The remains of what resembles the foundation of a barn sit close to the former home.

By most accounts, Hanton City became a ghost town in the early nineteenth century, but it was not completely unoccupied until well into the twentieth century. The Daniel family lived in a house on Rocky Hill, a mile into the woods from Douglas Pike and Rocky Hill Road. The house was constantly occupied from 1936 until the 1950s, when the family finally moved out. The house had no running water or electricity. Water was drawn from a well near the home, and light was provided by the aid of kerosene lamps. After the family moved away, they used it as a summer home until it was mysteriously set on fire and burned in 1972. For many years, all that

Corncrib mounts along the side of a trail in Hanton City. *Photo courtesy of Jim Ignasher.*

remained was the massive cellar, which was filled in around 2005. When you reach the spot where the cellar hole was, a fork in the road will take you toward the best sites in the ruined village, including the threshing rock and what is considered the center of the old town.

The other family to live in the Hanton City woods was the Wilcoxes. They lived there only briefly, from around 1927 until World War II. The Wilcox site is one of the first to be seen while walking up the trail from Decotis Farm Road. A 1947 map shows the home site labeled "unoccupied," meaning that the buildings were still standing and probably in a habitable condition. This same map also shows the home of J.J. Daniel on the rough Rumbly of Hanton City.

There are a few poems and stories of Hanton City and what life was like there. The poems were handed down from generation to generation, retold as the orators heard them from their parents before:

Widow Mack and Short Ann Free
Tanner Ben and Sim Bushee

And:

> *Up in Hanton City*
> *There lived a very tall man.*
> *He had a handsome daughter*
> *And her name was Hittean*
> *She was courted by Lords & Dukes,*
> *And by many a wealthy Knight.*
> *But no one but Philip the Darkey*
> *Could gain her heart's delight.*

There were once rumors of old people who really knew what happened to Hanton City. When queried they would only answer with silence.

"So there really was a Hanton City?"

"Yup."

"And it disappeared, did it?"

"Ayeh."

Although there is no hunting, some still disregard the posts, so be sure to wear bright colors when traversing the trails, just in case and obey all posted signs.

The Witch Tree, Smithfield

A short detour off Route 44 at the intersection of Mann School Road and Colwell Road sits a local legend. Right smack in the middle of the intersection is a tree. It is a replacement for the original, which had a creepy legend to it. The tree was also the cause of several automobile fatalities over the years. These deaths and other incidents have sparked the idea of the tree being haunted and cursed.

The tree was once a well-known landmark for travelers along the back roads of the town. When giving directions to a traveler unfamiliar with the roads, one would say, "When you get to the tree, take a left and follow the road from there."

The tree got its name due to one legend that states it is haunted by a witch that lived nearby. When her home burned down, her soul sought refuge in the tree, wreaking havoc on those who dared come too close to the old oak. She is not the only one who inhabits the tree.

Many who drove past the oak at night have sworn they saw the ghosts of young children standing in front of the old tree. Legend trippers have often played the "Witch Tree Game," driving around the tree three times (some say the number is thirteen) counterclockwise in hopes that the ghosts would appear. A ghostly biker has been known to suddenly appear at the tree and follow automobiles down the road, pulling alongside them before vanishing into thin air.

The old tree bore many scars from those who failed to negotiate the intersection. Over time, the tree began to fall apart, yet it still stood ominously in the middle of the road until it was finally cut down. The town replaced it with a new tree surrounded by a stone wall. If you decide to trek out to the intersection, be mindful and look for passing motorists, both real and not.

The Mysterious Skeleton of Route 44, Greenville

Historian Jim Ignasher of Smithfield dug up this interesting piece of macabre history. There is a small restaurant and lounge—as of this writing, called Frank and John from Italy—just before Waterman Lake on Route 44. It is very easy to spot as it is right on the side of the road. There are a few homes next to it. On April 11, 1977, one of those homeowners was digging out a stump next to the garage when he uncovered a human skull. After examining the situation, he immediately called the police, who filed a report, "The skull had a full set of teeth and appeared to be that of a human. It was found approximately 3–4 feet down in the ground and 20 feet from the west corner of the garage."

It was also concluded that the skull was very old and had been in the ground a long time. There were no known cemeteries in that area, and further investigation turned up none of the wood fragments or nails that would have been present with a coffin burial. The police also found several more bones, leading them to believe a whole body was buried there. The medical examiner's office came and took the remains for evaluation, but in the meantime, detectives had to determine who it was and when and why they died.

Records of the property held no clues, but one elderly citizen stated that a "sick house" once graced the land. These were places where those who became ill with contagious diseases were brought to keep them away from the general populace. Could this person have died in the sick house?

On April 13, two days after the discovery, the *Evening Bulletin* reported that the medical examiner's preliminary findings showed the bones to be those of a young woman. It was also concluded she had been in the ground no more than fifty years. She had no jewelry, and her bones showed signs of foul play. Further examinations revealed that the remains belonged to a White female, between twelve and sixteen, who stood approximately four feet, ten inches tall. The report went on to state that the young woman was "probably in good health" and that X-rays didn't show any signs of disease or injury that would indicate foul play. Unfortunately, the report did not narrow down the time of death or state a cause.

The findings are not consistent with someone dying in a sick house. To this day, the mystery of the woman's identity remains unsolved. Perhaps, as Jim Ignasher stated, "The answers still lie buried with the rest of her bones under a driveway on Putnam Pike."

Note: While there, stop in the restaurant and have a refreshment. You may want to ask about the ghosts that roam within. A house was once attached to the side and burned down. The place was, a very long time ago, a rough-and-tumble roadhouse where several tragic incidents took place. Also, many years ago, an automobile went off the road and into the lake. For six months, it went unnoticed until the waters receded, exposing the vehicle and its driver.

Glocester

Leaving Smithfield, Route 44 continues westward through the town of Glocester. Glocester was once much larger, until 1806, when the north portion was annexed and called Burrillville, after nineteenth-century United States senator and Rhode Island attorney general James Burrill Jr.

The town is primarily rural, and Chepachet is its main village. The name "Chepachet" is local Indian for "devil's bag" or "devil's bag place." According to Dr. Usher Parsons, in his 1861 book *Indian Names of Places in Rhode Island,*

> *A bag or wallet was found there, probably dropped by some hunter, and as no one could tell who, an Indian said it was the Devil. Hence, Chepuck, devil; chak, bag; now converged into "Chepachet." Since, according to Parsons, "the final et in many Indian names means place," the name is rightfully "Devil bag place."*

The small village center has, for the most part, defied time and progress. This may be the reason so many spirits remain in the antiquated structures.

Route 44, Chepachet Center. Note the strange white mist behind the trolley. *Author's collection.*

UFO over 44, Chepachet

In 2001, two friends driving east along Route 44 in Chepachet, Rhode Island, witnessed an object hovering above the tree line. The two followed the object, turning off the road directly under it. It was a dark metal sphere with circulating lights along the edge. When the two rolled down their window to get a better look, the sphere shot off into the sky and instantly vanished.

Tavern on Main, Chepachet

One of the most haunted places to visit along Route 44 sits right in the center of Chepachet and has become legendary for its paranormal activity.

The Tavern on Main was built in 1760 as a private home. It became a business establishment in 1799 when Cyrus Cooke turned it into a tavern and inn. Cooke's tavern served as a stage stop along the Putnam Pike (Route 44) from Providence, Rhode Island, to Hartford, Connecticut. Travelers dined and lodged while fresh horses were exchanged for the next leg of the route. The food at the tavern is exquisite, as it has been through the centuries. This excellent cuisine, coupled with its antique furnishings, makes an irresistible atmosphere for all, including the several ghosts that remain long after their mortal frames have turned to dust.

The tavern first gained its notoriety when a peddler named Acotes came to Chepachet with a sack full of merchandise for sale. He checked into the inn but never checked out. The following day, the unfortunate peddler was found murdered on the back steps of the tavern. He was buried east of the inn on a hill, in a cemetery that now bears his name.

The tavern was also the focus of one of Rhode Island's most controversial political battles. In 1842, Thomas Dorr was elected governor of Rhode Island under the People's Party. When he attempted to take his seat, the incumbent governor, Samuel King, refused to step down, asserting that the party was illegitimate—and therefore, the election was as well. A rebellion ensued. King's troops marched toward Chepachet, and the Dorr army encamped on Acotes Hill. When Dorr saw he was vastly outnumbered, he dispersed his troops and fled to nearby Connecticut. Some of Dorr's men set up a defensive outpost in the tavern, which also served as Dorr's headquarters during his endeavor to become governor. King's troops rallied outside the windows, guns drawn, ready to fire, while Dorr's men stood inside with their guns trained on King's men. Innkeeper Jedediah Sprague jumped through a window and managed to prevent the impending skirmish. The only casualty from the rebellion took place inside the tavern when one of King's troops fired a shot through the door's keyhole, hitting Horace Borden (Bardeen) in the thigh. King's troops lodged at the tavern for the summer, nearly bankrupting the owner, Jedediah Sprague, as he was never compensated by the state for their gluttonous leisure.

As time passed, the tavern took on many roles—boardinghouse, offices and billiards hall, to name a few. In the mid- to late twentieth century, the establishment acquired a seedy reputation, as fights and other violence became commonplace within its walls. This period may have left some scars on the atmosphere of the building that linger to this day. Howard Phillips Lovecraft indicated in his letters that he sojourned at the tavern during his journeys to Pascoag and West Glocester's Dark Swamp in search of a creature called "IT."

Among the ghosts of the tavern are a woman seen in the right rear booth of the dining room, a man thought to be Thomas Dorr, another woman who is either sad or angry or both, a few former employees and owners and a child seen everywhere in the establishment.

The ghost of the woman occasionally seen in the right rear booth of the dining room by staff and patrons alike is called Alice. Gene Waterman owned the tavern from 1982 to 2004. He experienced a lot of unexplained

The extremely haunted Tavern on Main in Chepachet holds several spirits. *Author's collection.*

phenomena during his tenure as tavern keeper. Alice made her presence known to Gene numerous times. In a *Northwest Neighbors* article from 2003, Gene personally described her as wearing colonial attire, as if she was "dressed for a picnic or a party," while she appeared to be waiting for someone to join her.

Another spirit is that of a little boy who is seen and heard in every room of the restaurant. One afternoon, an employee of the gas station next door and his wife witnessed the little boy looking out the taproom window. The wife approached the window to see why a child would be in the taproom at that hour. As she neared the window, the figure backed away from the glass and vanished into the darkness. The strangest part of this account was that the tavern was vacant and locked up during the time of the sighting.

On one occasion, a tavern keeper entered the building, as was his usual routine, at about eleven thirty in the morning. As he turned on the dining room lights, he saw a young boy standing beside the old stove just outside the ladies' room. Fearing that someone might have left a child there overnight, he quickly asked the boy if he was all right. The boy then turned and walked through the wall next to the kitchen door.

A father and daughter dining at the tavern also met the little boy. The little girl had to use the restroom, and the father became concerned when she did not return after a few minutes. When he approached the door, he heard his daughter talking to someone in the ladies' room. He knocked on the door and inquired how she was. She answered she was OK and was "just talking to the little boy."

Thinking it improper for a little boy to be in the bathroom, the father opened the door. His daughter was standing in front of the sink, motioning to her side, where she said the boy was. She also stated that he wanted to come home with them. The father took their dinner to go and left the building in a hurry.

A woman taking an early lunch entered the dining room and proceeded toward the old coal stove where the daily soup and bread were laid out for customers to enjoy. She approached the stove and saw a boy standing in front of it. Thinking it was an employee's child, she began to converse with the lad. As she spoke to him, the boy faded away in front of her.

Although the ghost of the young child has been seen and heard on various occasions, the lad's identity remains a mystery.

Dave and Kristen Lumnah took the helm of the tavern in early 2007. Since then, the ghostly occurrences have increased to the point where there is a new story to tell every week. The frequency of bizarre incidents has made the tavern arguably the most haunted place in the region.

One year, Dave asked neighboring Brown & Hopkins Country Store staff members Liz and Barbara to decorate the tavern for the season. The two were hanging red, white and blue bunting on the walls upstairs. Barbara was up on a ladder arranging one swath under a portrait, and Liz was in the opposite corner of the room doing the same. Liz suddenly heard Barbara say, "Oh no, it's all set. I got it."

Liz asked what she needed, and Barbara, realizing Liz was on the other side of the room, screamed, "Oh my God! I just felt somebody push my arm! I thought it was you trying to help me!"

Debra Marks, a longtime tavern employee, has had many experiences ranging from water turning on in the bathroom by itself to hearing her name called while alone in the taproom. She and her sister Chris are well acquainted with the spirits of the tavern. Chris remembers one now-famous incident regarding a television sitting over the bar's end. One evening, a regular was standing below the television, stating in front of a full bar that he did not believe the tavern was haunted and the stories were all bunk. Suddenly, everyone began shouting at him to move as the television lifted off its perch. Luckily, he was quick enough to avoid being hit as it crashed to the floor. When called in to investigate, authors Tom D'Agostino and Arlene

Nicholson, on close inspection, revealed that the dust on the shelf had not been disturbed, meaning that the television was lifted from its resting place and did not slide off the shelf. The unit suffered some case cracks but still worked fine. As for the skeptic, he was instantly converted.

The ghosts of the tavern vary in era and personality. They are remnants of those who either passed through town or had made the building an essential part of their lives. From the little boy to the woman in the rear booth and the other restless spirits, all seem to be attracted to the people who come to the tavern to wine and dine. Perhaps they are just attempting to mingle with the patrons or have something they wish to relate. The energy in the tavern is strong, intense yet pleasing, making it the perfect place for a haunting. The website www.tavernonmainri.com even has a video of a ghost taken during one of our investigations in 2006. The footage shows what appears to be a ghost in very old-fashioned garb getting up from one of the tables and walking toward the back of the room where the kitchen door is. The footage was captured on a young investigator's camera, and although we tried to recreate it numerous times, we have yet to rationally explain what was captured on film. We can only surmise at this point that it was someone from long ago still biding their time at the tavern.

Old Stone Mill Antiques, Chepachet

Old Stone Mill Antiques at 1169 Putnam Pike in Chepachet, Rhode Island, has some of the most interesting finds around as well as a few interesting ghosts.

Lawton Owen built the mill in 1814 for the Chepachet Manufacturing Company. The structure stood three stories high from the street level, with a gabled roof and belfry. Owen's mill produced cotton cloth until Sayles and Smith gained control in 1864. The new owners introduced wool to the process of creating cassimere and satinet.

After the Great Freshet of 1867, the third floor and gabled roof were removed and a flat roof was laid down, making the structure smaller and stronger. The business grew, as did the size of the mill. At one point, the building was four times the size of what it is today. The original stone section was the picker mill, a dangerous and unhealthy place to work. Children employed in the mill often met tragic fates while working the unforgiving machines or repairing broken threads on the looms. The mill

Stone Mill Antiques on Route 44 in Chepachet.

later became the Glocester Yarn Company before finally closing its doors in 1969 after 155 years of manufacturing. In 1982, the wooden additions were demolished for safety reasons, leaving the original stone section of the mill still standing.

Although several proprietors subsequently owned the mill, Debra McCarron was the one who felt an uncanny connection with the building from the first time she drove by the then-vacant building. In a personal interview, Debra once stated, "I remember driving by this place many times saying to myself; 'I am going to own that building one day.'"

Many years later, when the building went up for sale, Debra was able to fulfill her dream and purchase the old mill. From there, renovations began, but it was not long before those working on the upgrades found out they were not the only ones tenanting the place. During renovations, the scampering of footsteps and the giggling of a child were occasionally heard on the second floor.

On one occasion, Deb went upstairs to arrange some of the antiques. As she started turning off the lights, she came face-to-face with the glowing form of a little boy. The misty figure reached out its hand in her direction. It startled Deb, but she was not so much frightened as curious about

The main floor of Old Stone Mill Antiques in Chepachet.

what the child wanted. She stood there and stared in half disbelief at the glowing apparition. It finally faded away in front of her. Deb stated that on many occasions, she feels that someone is in the building with her. Many customers have come down the stairs perplexed by the fact that they heard footsteps behind them and turned around, only to find they were the only ones there.

People shopping for antiques in the building have confided in Deb that they could feel something in certain areas. The spirits are not a threat; rather, they're happy the mill is being used for such a purpose. Debra alluded, "It seems they just want to let us know that they are here and are not trying to scare us but are happy we are here with them."

A regular customer often has run-ins with the ghost of a little girl. When he is upstairs looking around, the child ghost tugs on his shirtsleeve to get his attention. Once, the man told Deb that the girl was motioning for him to play hide and seek with her. Perhaps he resembles someone she was close to during her lifetime.

No one has been able to find the identities of the ghosts that reside in the mill and like to make their presence known. Perhaps they are happy that it is an antique shop where they may be more at home with the fashions and trends of their time.

The village has candlelight shopping on the three Thursdays before Christmas. Depending on the time, you can hear the laughter and footsteps of the living passing through looking for that perfect gift, but later, when the crowds dwindle and the candles burn down…

Gloucester Light Infantry Armory on Dorr Drive, Chepachet

The armory on Dorr Drive, directly off Route 44 behind the town hall, was once part of a schoolhouse. A section of the building burned down long ago, and the remaining portion of the historic building now houses the Gloucester Light Infantry's equipment. It also houses a former student who met with tragedy many years ago.

While the building was being used as a schoolhouse, students were obliged to attend their daily lessons. One day, a student left the building in a hurry, bolting across Dorr Drive into Douglas Hook Road without looking to see if any horses or wagons were coming down the road. Unfortunately, a carriage traveling toward the main pike struck the youth, running him over and killing him.

Witnesses, including some of the infantry reenactment crew, have seen the visage of the boy emerging from the building and running out into the street before vanishing into thin air. The building is easy to spot as it can be seen from Route 44 and Douglas Hook Road.

Acotes Hill Cemetery, Chepachet

Acotes Hill Cemetery is haunted by the ghost of a peddler who was found murdered on the back stairs of the old Stagecoach Tavern (presently Tavern on Main). Because his religious denomination was unknown, he was taken to the hill entering the village and buried on the western edge. This hill would later play host to the decisive scene during the Dorr Rebellion of 1842, when Thomas Dorr set up a fort and troops there. A 1937 Rhode Island travel guide mentions a Dorr memorial on the top of Acotes Hill. The area later became a burial ground for all denominations. Many historical cemeteries were relocated to Acotes when it became necessary to move them. People often attest to seeing the ghost of an ancient peddler wandering about the top of the hill near his unmarked grave.

Another great tale from Acotes Cemetery is that of Arnold Staples. Staples, a retired Smithfield undertaker, decided to dig his own grave. In 1911, the eighty-nine-year-old man shoveled out a plot himself to make sure it was to his liking. His wife died on December 10, 1877, and Staples, being a sentimental sort, decided to brave the elements and dig the frozen ground on that same day in 1911. Not long after he completed his task, heavy rains caved the hole in, forcing poor Arnold to dig his final resting place once again. This time, he fortified the hole with supports to keep the grave from collapsing. Staples died on July 1, 1913, and was buried next to his wife in the grave he had twice dug for himself.

This interment did not last as long as he would have expected, for in 1934, family members had his remains, along with those of his wife and children, removed to Acotes Cemetery in Chepachet. Staples is listed in the Rhode Island Cemetery records as interred in Smithfield Cemetery SM084 and Glocester Cemetery GL023. So Mr. Staples is recorded as buried in two different places and had three graves dug to rest in peace.

The cemetery hours are posted on the gate, which is locked after closing.

Brown & Hopkins General Store, Chepachet

Brown & Hopkins General Store is said to be the oldest continually running store of its kind in the United States. In 1799, Timothy Wilmarth built the structure as a private home. When Ira Evans purchased the home in 1809, he turned it into a general store. James Brown and William Hopkins owned the store from 1921 to 1964 before the Steere family took ownership, leaving the name unchanged. In 2004, Elizabeth Yuill purchased the store, keeping the centuries-old tradition alive. B&H boasts old-fashioned delights, events, handmade items and many other products that bring the customer back to times when life was simple and slower.

Being a former home, the building has several permanent residents still letting everyone know they are there to stay. One particular ghost is that of a woman the staff calls Ella. Staff member Bonnie Godin, has experienced Ella a few times on all three floors of the building, as she shared in an interview for this book:

I was working over here (in the back room on the first floor), and I felt a very cold breeze. I thought it was the air conditioner, so I moved, but when I moved, the air followed me, and the hair on my neck went up. I was talking

Gifts and ghosts abound at Brown & Hopkins Country Store.

to a lady, and she asked, "Who else is here?" And she makes a gesture of a ghost. So I tell her about the bedroom and the fireplace where they are most active. The lady then says, "There is something that is following you right here, right now." She then stated that whatever it was that was in here with me was not comfortable with her, and it wanted to be near me.

Bonnie also saw a shadow cross the wall on the third floor while she was the only person up there at the time. Bonnie remembers a man and woman mentioning the presence of a little girl with long black hair and blue eyes who died of a respiratory illness in one of the bedrooms. The little girl is called Abigail by the staff.

When employees enter the store in the morning, they often find certain items in complete disarray, such as scarves or hats that appear to have been tried on and discarded during the late hours of the night. Voices are heard around the rooms that are uninhabited by humans, and footsteps resound on the second and third floors when they are otherwise empty. A few of the staff have heard people upstairs milling around after closing time, but on ascending the only staircase to let their customers know it was past store hours, not one living soul was found anywhere. The ghost of a man is also present in one of the rooms on the second floor that was probably once his bedroom.

Staff members Warren Usey, Callie Bisset, Cindy Carroll and Cynthia Maciel have had experiences while working in the store. Warren actually saw Ella standing in a corner one day, just staring back at him. "She was standing in the corner just watching me," he said in an interview with the authors.

He always says good morning to Ella, although "she never says good morning back." The staff gets a tingling feeling and feels a cold breeze just before Ella makes her presence known. Warren also mentioned the man in the bedroom upstairs. "I never really noticed him, but others have. I can't imagine he is happy with all the people that pass through there."

A few women shopping on the second floor descended the stairs while two other customers headed upstairs. One of them was overheard by staff saying, "If you are going up there, I'd be careful. I am not surprised this place is haunted. We heard someone talking and walking around in the old bedroom, but no one was in the room when we entered."

The ghosts like to show their presence in mirrors. Mirrors are thought to be portals for spirits to enter the world of the living, and at Brown & Hopkins, they are not shy about using them.

Brown & Hopkins is located at 1179 Putnam Pike (Route 44) in Chepachet Center. All kinds of events take place there at different times of the year, so check out the website at www.shopbrownandhopkins.com.

Town Trader Antiques, Chepachet

Town Trader Antiques at 1177 Putnam Pike (Route 44) was once a 1690s trading post and is the oldest structure in Chepachet center. The building features hand-hewn beams and a flueless beehive brick fireplace in the center of the oldest part of the building. It was also home to Lydia Slocum, the birthplace of Rhode Island attorney general Ziba Slocum and the home of Charles Carlton, a Spanish-American War veteran. The building is home to a ghost that owner Charlie Wilson calls the "First Lady of the house." He believes this may be Lydia Slocum. The Slocum family lived in the newer portion of the building from around the 1780s until the 1950s.

Wilson, who bought the building in 2005, also lives on the upper floor of the building, so he is in constant company with the entity that haunts the place. The first time he saw her, it happened so fast, he was unprepared for it. A white silhouette appeared out of nowhere and just floated on by.

While renovating the attic, a beam gave way, and Charlie fell through, landing on his back on the first floor. When he opened his eyes, he saw

The former owner still watches over Town Trader Antiques on Route 44 in Chepachet.

the ghost of a woman looking down at him. He feels she may have helped cushion his landing, as he was not injured in the least.

Charlie has a kitchen table with four chairs. He pushes three of them into the table and leaves one chair pushed out enough so that when he goes upstairs for the night, he can just seat himself right away if his hands are full. Every night, he notices someone has pushed the chair in. He thinks it is the lady of the house tidying up.

Others have seen the ghost or have felt the presence of something while in the store. During an interview for this book, Charlie related,

> *Many people that walk in here, especially in the winter time when I have the heat on in the building, will feel a cold draft following them and will say, "You have a ghost in here, I can feel the presence."*

Whoever is there, whether it be Mrs. Slocum or someone else, is not harmful but rather helpful. The store is full of treasures from another time, as are the ghosts.

Town Trader Antiques is located at 1177 Putnam Pike (Route 44) next to Brown & Hopkins General Store. To check out the store online, go to thetowntrader.com.

Cady's Tavern:
Rhode Island's Original Roadhouse, West Glocester

Cady's Tavern in West Glocester, Rhode Island, has been a town landmark since 1810 when Hezekiah Cady opened the stagecoach stop as a resting place for travelers along the Putnam/Providence Pike. Horses were changed while the driver and passengers refreshed themselves with food and drink. Sometime during the 1920s, a fire destroyed the building (some argue it was the barn and not the inn that burned). The remains of the structure can be seen in the woods across from the present Cady's.

Cady's boasts live entertainment, a friendly atmosphere, a full bar, a pub fare menu and a few resident ghosts. Incidents include chairs and dishes being thrown by an unseen entity, voices coming from the rooms upstairs, the ghost of a little boy appearing in the ballroom and a host of other strange events that cannot be readily explained. One of the cooks was in the kitchen preparing a meal when all the pans flew off the shelf at once. Owner Robin Tyo stated that such incidents are common in the old tavern.

Robin has had several paranormal groups investigate the building because of its activity. One of the more frequent occurrences is the spirit of a child giggling and opening the door to the ballroom on the second floor. The ghost was seen a few times by some of the staff and patrons and the giggling recorded. The ballroom is relegated to storage, but once overflowed with music and dance of a bygone era.

Circa 1810 Cady's Tavern.

The latch on the door between an upstairs room and the ballroom often lifts as if someone is about to exit the room, yet no one appears in the doorway. The second floor used to be an apartment. In that area, the ethereal voices of a male adult and one of a female adult were captured on a recorder.

Some old photographs and newspaper clippings of the building are neatly preserved in a folder for all to peruse on request. An old signboard in the ballroom from years ago says the tavern was established in 1810. Patrons visiting the upstairs rooms have heard that date whispered in the air after inquiring how old the place is.

The main room is not without paranormal activity. Bar stools move and voices are heard when no one is in the room.

Cady's is known as Rhode Island's original roadhouse and rightly so. With live entertainment, open microphone nights, blues jams and great food, it is no wonder the ghosts stick around.

Cady's Tavern is located at 2168 Putnam Pike; visit cadystavern.com.

Just before the border of Connecticut, Route 96 veers off to the left. It is there you will find a place called Dark Swamp within the Durfee Hill Management Area, where a strange creature has existed for centuries, roaming the gloomy parcel of woods so aptly named…

IT, West Glocester

In August 1923, Howard Phillips Lovecraft and his best friend, Clifford Martin Eddy, took a trolley from their hometown of Providence to the center of Chepachet, a small but thriving village in Glocester. It was their intention to discover the exact whereabouts of a hideous creature the locals knew only by the name IT.

The monster lived in an area about halfway between the village and the Putnam, Connecticut border in a place called Dark Swamp. According to legend, the sun's warming rays never reached the ground of this murky piece of land. The trees, with their coarse, gnarly limbs, intermingled with each other, creating a vast web of twisted branches that made entrance or egress almost impossible. It was there that IT made its home, emerging from the swamp whenever it sought to feed. No other living creatures dared venture close to the habitat of IT, instinctively knowing that doom awaited them there. The people of the area were careful to chop their wood, hunt and fish far from the boundaries of the swamp for fear they might be seen by IT and never live to tell of the ordeal.

Lovecraft and his traveling companion inquired about the creature with little result, save for some of the old-timers who knew the legend from previous generations. The two trekked down Route 44, past Cady's Tavern to where Elbow Rock Road and Route 94 lie. A few folks there knew some stories and were glad to share them. Unfortunately, Lovecraft and Eddy never found the lair or signs of the monster, but the trip did serve the two well. They would later use the legend and their experience in several of their stories. How did they come to know of this creature in the first place? Perhaps it was the account by local pirate Albert Hicks or a later account by Neil Hopkins that sparked their curiosity.

Albert Hicks was born in Foster, Rhode Island, in 1820. His father was a farmer, and it seemed he was to follow the same course, but unfortunately for him, his wild and reckless demeanor steered him clear of any honest livelihood. At a young age, he turned to robbery, piracy and murder. While still working on his father's farm, Hicks heard about some treasure Captain Kidd might have hidden near the Paine Farm. Some years later, Hicks and a few of his cronies decided to test the legend.

One moonless night, John Jepp, Ben Cobb, Ben Saunders, all from Glocester and Hicks crept into the far field of the farm and began digging for the loot. Suddenly they were accosted by a terrible being Hicks later described as a large beast with eyes of fire the size of pewter bowls. When it breathed, flames came out of its mouth and nostrils, scorching the brush as it passed. It was as large as a cow, with dark wings on each side and spiral horns like a ram's protruding from its head. Its feet were much like a duck's but measured a foot and a half across. The beast's body was covered with scales the size of clam shells that rattled as it moved along. The "thing" had light emanating from its sides like a lantern. Even before they saw the beast, they became aware of its presence, as it gave off the smell of burning wool. The beast came out of nowhere and stood before them. All four men dropped their picks and shovels and ran in fright, never to return. Albert Hicks was later convicted of murder and piracy in New York and hanged for the crime, one of the last New England pirates to be executed for their vocation.

The next account appeared in the *Evening Hour* on January 15, 1896. Neil Hopkins of Glocester, Rhode Island, was walking home from his work in Putnam, Connecticut, when in the darkest portion of the road in front of him, a strange beast appeared. As Hopkins took flight, the beast began to chase him. He could not discern exactly what the creature was but confirmed that it was some supernatural beast living in the forest near Dark Swamp, where the chase originated.

According to the article, Hopkins later told neighbors that the monster was as large as an elephant but with no tail and "seemed to be all a-fire and had a hot breath." The creature also gave off a metallic sound as it ran; he described it as "steel against steel."

The strange beast chased Hopkins for a short distance before bounding back into the woods. Hopkins could hear it breaking branches and crunching twigs as it lumbered off into the void. The people of the village were sure it was the same creature that scared Hicks and his men half a century before.

Is the beast called IT still lurking in the woods of West Glocester? There are some who still believe that something resides eternally in the area of Dark Swamp, waiting for an unwary traveler to enter its domain.

CHAPTER 3

CONNECTICUT

PUTNAM TO HARTFORD, 57.01 MILES (91.75 KM)

Putnam

Putnam came to be an incorporated town in 1855, taken from parts of Killingly, Pomfret and Thompson. The area was originally known as Aspinock and later renamed in honor of Revolutionary War general Israel Putnam. This little mill town sits on the border of Rhode Island. It resembles a small Vermont town with its waterfall, antiquated homes and shops and old mills that have found new life and purpose. Although small in size, it is large in history, once considered the hub of travel between cities like Hartford, Worcester, Boston and New York. It also is worth the trip to see some of the most famous and bizarre haunts in the region.

The Bradley Playhouse

The historic Bradley Playhouse sits at 30 Front Street (Route 44) at the entrance of the center of town, like a beacon of the artistic culture Putnam has become known for. It is a charming theater where live performances fill the air with magic as actors entertain the audience with their talents. There are also the permanent occupants that sometimes entertain, or even scare, the living within.

The theater, designed and constructed by local architect Charles H. Kelley, opened its doors on January 29, 1901. Owner Ramson Bradley hosted vaudeville shows, silent movies, sound movies and live performances. The theater was victim to three fires, two in 1914, just fourteen hours apart, and one on December 9, 1937. The building had a specially designed asbestos curtain that would drop in front of the stage, containing the conflagration to that area alone. The curtain, one of three known to have served its purpose, worked during the original fires, and the building sustained minimal damages. Over the course of its life, the theater was expanded and improved. On December 25, 1937, the playhouse began showing first-run movies. The name was later changed to the Imperial and ran under that designation until 1985. The name was changed back to the Bradley Playhouse with the inception of the Northeast Repertory Company bringing live acting back to its stage. The Bradley Playhouse once held one thousand guests but eventually was reduced to a four-hundred-seat-capacity due to renovations, larger seats and other modern comforts.

The Bradley is presently under the auspices of Theatre of Northeastern Connecticut Inc., an amateur community group that produces eight main shows a year along with various fundraisers. The group members are no strangers to the ghosts that inhabit the building. Strange noises echo through the theater often, causing the actors to take a second look about the hall. Seats are known to move as if someone is either getting up or moving them to get through an aisle. People have seen shadows pass behind them; some lean forward to give the audience member extra passing room, yet when they turn around, there is no physical being creating the mysterious shadow.

During one particular play, a coffin was used as a prop. Lying on top of the coffin was a sash and a rose. Just before showtime, the rose disappeared from the coffin lid. Since it was an important prop for the upcoming scene, the cast and crew searched frantically for the flower but came up short. It was decided that until another rose could be procured, they would have to improvise with another prop. When they carried the prop over to the coffin, the rose, which had been missing, was once again in the exact same spot where it had been originally placed. No one could have taken or replaced it, as the coffin had been in plain view of the cast and crew.

During several shows, a man in an old-fashioned suit with short-cut facial hair appeared in a seat near the back of the building. No one saw him enter or sit down or noticed anything strange until he dissipated in front of astonished attendees.

One of the most common occurrences is the appearance of a ghost named Victoria. The phantom figure, dressed in a flowing blue dress, is often seen in the balcony by performers during rehearsals. The spirit is dressed in 1940s clothing and, according to those who have witnessed her, does not care for any plays other than musicals; she becomes very agitated and leaves. She has also been witnessed backstage and in the basement. People in the building have heard footsteps when the place is otherwise empty and quiet. The floors have let out an unmistakable groan, as if someone is moving across them.

A man came to watch a show and had never heard any of the ghost stories. He arrived early and sat down in one of the front-row seats. A few moments later, the seat next to him folded down, yet there was no one seated in it. He then told the manager that he could feel his father's presence next to him. One staff member walked across the stage on her first day at the Bradley and immediately felt as if something was following her. Performers have felt some invisible being resting a hand on their shoulders while on stage. According to former playhouse manager Patricia Green, interviewed by the authors,

There is so much activity going on, not only spiritually but physically. There are about one hundred and twenty live bodies that bounce through here on a regular basis; the members, cast members and core group all with these incredibly dominant personalities that carry their energies around and bounce their creativity off of one another.

The energy and excitement of the theater is enough to keep anyone coming back. Some have just never left.

UFO over Putnam

On December 21, 1965, at 7:33 p.m., over Putnam, Connecticut, a Northeast Airlines pilot sighted an unknown round object that he later described as turning pink, then orange, then white in color, about the size of a quarter held at arm's length. The object passed directly in front of the plane, and after seven minutes, it picked up speed and disappeared. The pilot was flying a DC-6 aircraft at ten thousand feet on a heading of 260 degrees. The total length of the observation was eleven minutes.

Not all accounts of UFOs are archaic. Many modern-day UFO sightings attest that either someone is still visiting or people are confusing technological toys with visitors from outer space. In some cases, there can be no doubt that it may have not been of this world.

The White Ghost Train, Putnam

Nothing conjures up mystery like the thought of a phantom train floating along some old railroad tracks. The train in this case was called the Ghost Train for a slightly different reason. It was an actual train, and the label was given due to its shimmering white paint and gold trim.

The railroad tracks literally run through the center of Putnam, where trains once stopped to deliver or pick up goods and passengers. The system was part of the Airline Railroad, so called due to the imaginary line that was drawn through the air on a map to create the shortest possible train route from New York to Boston.

The White Train made its maiden run on March 16, 1891. From the engine to the last Pullman car, the train glistened in white and gold. The engineer and staff all wore white with gold bands, and the coal that fueled the locomotive was whitewashed at every stop. The train consisted of an engine, a coal car, seven parlor cars, four passenger coaches and two Pullman royal buffet smokers. It was truly the fast and wealthy way to travel for its day.

The train got its nickname, the Ghost Train, not only because of its color but also due to the fact that it ran mostly in the dark hours of the night. Making only one stop, it would reach its destination in record time, slowing down in Putnam to scoop water from a long trough located south of Mechanics Street before speeding off once again. Among the famous people who rode it were Charles Dickens and Rudyard Kipling. Kipling was so amazed by the train that he wrote a short story about it called "007."

The White Ghost, as it was also called, was a sight to behold, but it was not without its tragedies. In 1892, a fifteen-year-old boy in Willimantic, Connecticut, was killed when he jumped from another train into the path of the oncoming Ghost Train. In March of 1893, James Bailey and his daughter Rose were struck by the train in East Wallingford, Connecticut, while crossing the tracks with their sleigh on a late winter evening. According to witnesses at the scene, the sleigh was literally blown into pieces by the impact, and James was killed instantly. Rose survived the collision and eventually recovered.

On May 12, 1895, William Sargent of Portland, Connecticut, was "cut to pieces by cars" according to the *Penny Press* of Portland, when he was run over by the train a mile east of Portland Station. The engineer saw a man lying on the tracks but could not stop the speeding train in time. The train was discontinued on October 20, 1895. According to railroad executives, the train became too expensive to maintain and keep clean.

Now the train is but a fading memory, but perhaps sometimes, when the faint sound of a whistle blows and the rumbling of an engine passes, who knows? It might just be the ghost of the Ghost Train.

The Flood of 1955 and Simoniz Park, Putnam

Cargill Falls flows through the center of Putnam within the boundaries of the Putnam River Trail. The trail extends 1.4 miles between Arch Street and Providence Street. Along the trail, hikers can read about Putnam's railroad history and mills and the famous 1955 flood. Along the east bank of the Quinebaug River, there are remnants of what was once a neighborhood. Foundations, patios, bricks and staircases are among the remains of the homes that were washed away during the terrible flood.

From Route 44 to Arch Street, many of these ruins are visible. Some people walking the trail after dark have heard families whispering in the wind among the remains of the dwellings. Whether they are the sounds of nature deceiving the ear or the sounds of people past still living in what used to be their homes is unclear. One thing's for sure: the trail is worth the time to walk and explore. Bring a lunch and sit at one of the tables. Perhaps you may hear someone playing in what was once their backyard.

The Home with No Porch, Putnam/Pomfret Line

Here is one more interesting tidbit worth mentioning. On Route 44, near the border of Putnam and Pomfret, sits a home that has a strange story regarding its haunted past. The owners of the home were convinced their house was haunted by a malevolent spirit and sought help by way of a medium. This person told them that in order to appease the spirit, they had to remove their front porch. It appears the spirit of the home did not like the addition. The front porch was removed, and supposedly, the entity faded. A few well-known paranormal groups actually investigated the home to find out if it was still haunted. The house in question and its exact location remain anonymous due to the fact that it is private property.

The Tale of Rufus Malbone, Putnam

Just before the Pomfret line, on the right side of the road in a yard, sits an obelisk enveloped by a stone wall. This is the grave of Rufus Malbone and his horse, Dolly. Malbone, a former slave, earned not only his freedom but also absolute respect for his accomplishments from his fellow neighbors and friends.

Malbone was born in 1824. After the Civil War, he moved to rural Putnam and made a living buying, selling and bartering produce from local farms. Somewhere along the way, he acquired his beloved horse, Dolly. The two were seen everywhere, never leaving each other's side.

Malbone was also known for his immense strength. One day, when he was traveling with a friend, the hay wagon they were on suddenly shuddered and a wheel fell off. Malbone lifted the wagon with his bare hands while his

Goats ramble around the confines of the monument for Rufus Malbone and his horse, Dolly.

friend replaced the wheel. It is said he could hoist full barrels of apple cider onto wagons with no aid but his own strength. Many legends and tales about Malbone endure to this day. Unfortunately, his strength became his end.

In the fall of 1884, Malbone was driving his wagon filled with apples with Dolly pulling the load. One of the wheels came off, and the now-sixty-year-old Malbone got under the cart and lifted the wagon, sliding the wheel back into place. Unexpectedly, he fell unconscious and was discovered by passing travelers. Malbone went in and out of consciousness for several days before succumbing to a broken blood vessel on October 12, 1884. On his deathbed, he asked that Dolly be cared for and, on her death, be buried with him in the same grave so they could be together forever.

After Rufus Malbone was interred, Dolly became melancholy, disruptive and angry. No one could sell her because no one really owned her except Rufus. A committee was formed on what to do with Dolly, and it was sadly decided that she should join her master. A single shot sent Dolly tumbling into the grave that she and Rufus now eternally share.

While You Are There: Grove Street Cemetery, Putnam

Grove Street Cemetery is home to two very interesting stories. The first takes place in the center of the burial ground. It is a tall monument with a giant granite ball on top that appears to be spinning. The ball is about four feet in diameter and weighs roughly two tons. Despite its size and weight, the ball refuses to sit still.

Researchers from the University of Connecticut once performed a study on the phenomenon and came up with several theories. One was expansion from the sun's heat; another was water freezing under the ball. Perhaps it was a magnetic field pulling the ball or vibrations from the road causing it to move. None of these theories could be confirmed. The closest that may have applied was the *possibility* of the ice freezing under the ball and moving it. This, however, would not explain how it moves in the warmer months.

In the last several years, the ball has rotated about a foot horizontally and eight inches vertically.

The next story concerns one of Putnam's most illustrious characters, Phineas Gardner Wright. Phineas was born on April 3, 1829, in Fitzwilliam, New Hampshire. His family moved to Woodstock, Connecticut, when he was but two years of age. At about age twenty-five, he moved to Putnam and became a somewhat wealthy man. Because he did not trust the local banks,

Grove Street Cemetery's mysterious rotating ball.

he would travel to Boston—horse, buggy and money—to do his banking there. In the early 1900s business directory, he is basically quoted as saying under "business," "Minding my own."

"Gard," as he was called, cared nothing for the modern conveniences of the times. Automobiles were smelly and noisy. Modern styles of clothing were not to his taste, and the din of the modern world often made him cringe with anger. Gard preferred the calm, peaceful serenity of Putnam—except the noise of the trains, from which he made a portion of his income.

Twelve years before his death, Gard decided to have a grand monument made for the family burial plot. The monument was written up in almost every conceivable magazine, gaining fame from Maine to California. When uncovered, the monument bore the bust of Mr. Wright coming out of one side of the stone—whiskers, watch fob and all—with a simple epitaph, "Going but know not where." As for the inscription, according to Ruth Flagg in her book *Phineas Gardner Wright: The Man and His Monument*, Wright had this to offer: "Them's true words, but there ain't many folks what's got the honesty or the courage to say the same thing."

Wright was displeased with the sculptor's poetic liberty in parting his whiskers, as was the custom of the time. He ordered the monument taken back to Worcester, where the parted beard could be removed and replaced with a fuller one. This was done, and Gard was happy once again.

As far as the grave was concerned, Gard had it dug extra wide and lined with brick so the earth would not crowd him in when his time came. One final detail worth noting is the fact that he filled the grave with liquor so when the time came to bury him, those in charge of the task could refresh themselves with libations. He also requested that, when he died, an inscription be carved on the stone, "Never beat by man, but by woman."

Phineas G. Wright passed away on May 2, 1918, at the age of eighty-nine, one of the oldest residents in Putnam. Over five hundred people attended his funeral, and he was buried in the family plot that sits along the outer road of the Grove Street Cemetery along Route 12.

To get to the cemetery, take route 44 into the center of Putnam, then bear left onto Route 12. Follow Route 12 for about half a mile, and the cemetery will be on the right. Please obey all posted rules and regulations.

Pomfret

The land that is now Pomfret was once called Mashmuket or Mashamoquet. It was settled in 1686 and incorporated in 1713, named after Pontefract in West Yorkshire, England. The town has a rural setting reminiscent of small towns in Vermont or Maine. Route 44 runs through Pomfret, lending the sightseer wonderful scenery and interesting places to stop and wander about. Old-fashioned stores, farms and other sites await the traveler, as well as a few well-known haunts.

Grill 37, Pomfret

Grill 37 on Route 44 in Pomfret has an illustrious history and active haunts. Built in 1765, it was originally the home of Lemuel Grosvenor. On November 7, 1795, George Washington appointed him postmaster. Lemuel's home was the first post office from New York to Boston, and he proudly served his appointment for forty years. Lemuel was born on August 11, 1752, and died on January 19, 1833. He married Eunice Putnam, daughter of famous general Isreal Putnam, on September 7, 1783. After Eunice's death in 1799, he married Sarah Perkins on March 9, 1801. He is buried in the Pomfret Street Cemetery on Route 44, a few miles away from his former home.

The building also served as a doctor's office, a private residence and, later, a restaurant known as the Harvest before becoming Grill 37. Grill 37 is hailed by many as the best steakhouse in Connecticut, but it also has a wide range of other menu delights. Whether you love seafood, pasta or vegetarian fare, they have it all. They also have a long history with ghosts that they are not afraid to talk about.

The ghost of a child has been witnessed in the doorway to the upstairs by staff and guests over the years. The taproom area is where people have witnessed items moving or found them on the floor where they could not have possibly just fallen on their own. Shadows moving about the building and the apparition of a man walking past the main dining room windows are just some of the building's permanent residents.

Debbi Farquhar, co-owner Ian's mom, helps with the family business and set up a special room with her late husband's Freemason items on the walls. In this room, the lights often flicker when she enters. She feels it is a sign that he is still watching over his family. In an interview with the authors, Debbi shared this story.

> The room that was once the original kitchen, now a dining room, is decorated with my late husband's Masonic apron, gloves, awards and medals. Whenever I go into the room, the lights flicker. I can feel his presence very strongly all around the room. The lights never flicker unless I enter the room.

Disembodied voices in the kitchen and dining rooms are also common. The porch dining room is where people have seen a misty form moving about. Repair people and other outside workers sometimes refuse to enter the building because of the activity inside. Several investigative groups have gathered plenty of evidence to prove that the building is haunted. The establishment holds many events during the year, including a convention for science fiction and horror buffs. Debbi also shared this account that stuck out in her mind:

> One evening, the husband of a new server came into Grille 37 and took a seat at the bar while waiting for his wife to finish her shift. He knew the place had a reputation for being haunted and asked me to tell some "ghost stories."
>
> I told him a few and he curiously inquired if I could ask the ghosts to do something in front of him. I jokingly asked, "Can you show us that you are here?" All of a sudden, two of the six lights above the bar, the two

above our heads, went dark. All of them are on the same circuit so there was no way they could be turned off without all of them going out. It really unsettled him and he said, "OK, I believe you." I said, "I love you," and the lights came back on.

Connecticut Paranormal Research Team has investigated the restaurant on many occasions. Christine Peer emailed the authors of this book the following excerpt of their experiences at Grill 37.

In May 2019, several employees, customers, and vendors saw and heard things they could not explain. There are stories of paranormal activity from the former owner and employees at the Harvest Restaurant. Now under new ownership as Grill 37, the hauntings are still occurring. Nancy Atkinson, a former manager, was closing one night after everyone had left. She saw a young boy dressed in early-period clothing walk through the lounge and vanish in front of her eyes. She ran into the bathrooms to see if anyone was still in the building. The outside doors were locked, and her car was the only one left on the property. When she arrived home late at night, Nancy contacted Christine Peer, the Director of the Connecticut Paranormal Research Team. Nancy was shaken up and requested help to rule out that she and the other staff were imagining things.

Following is the summary of the Connecticut Paranormal Research Team's investigations of Grill 37:

Christine and her husband, Dan, spent several days interviewing employees about what they've witnessed. A few cooks reported seeing objects coming out of boxes and rolling across the floor, turning 90-degree angles as if following them. They also witnessed cups flying out of their plastic sleeves in the basement storage area, narrowly missing them. Staff members have also seen glasses fly from the overhead rack and cupboards. Others have even seen tableware tossed across the length of the bar.

Apparently, the spirits are not fond of country music playing in the lounge. The music will turn off or switch to a different channel and play older-style music. Staff members, while alone, would feel a poke or hear their names called. Finding no one else around or another employee telling them they didn't call them or hear anything. The day shift staff always thought the night staff was playing tricks on them as all the tables would be set each evening for the next day with glasses, silverware, and a small plate. However, when staff would come in to open, they would find glasses turned over and utensils on the floor or out of place. Each shift would blame the other. Little did they know it was none of them moving anything around.

In the office upstairs, the manager, when staying overnight during a snowstorm, witnessed the computer turn on at 3:00 a.m. The printer would start spitting blank papers across the floor; this happened so frequently that she did not get up to turn it off. She started telling the spirit to turn the computer back off. Just like that, it would turn off. A vendor stopped by one afternoon before the restaurant opened. While standing in the lounge waiting for the manager to return with a document, they witnessed an unplugged vacuum cleaner turn on in the middle of the room and start moving across the floor. As the manager came into the room and saw this, she had to chase after the vendor, who was walking quickly out the door, to give him the document. Several customers have claimed to see people dressed in early-period clothing going up the main staircase of the original part of the house or witnessing their glass move across their table away from them.

The Connecticut Paranormal Research Team partnered with Ryan O'Connor of O'Conchobhair Productions, LLC, on Memorial Day weekend of 2019 to film a paranormal investigation at Grill 37. Throughout the investigation, it appeared that the spirits at Grill 37 wanted to be heard. Lights came on by themselves in the office upstairs, formally used as a bedroom when the location was a residence. With the entire film crew and the Connecticut Paranormal Research Team in the lounge area, Daniel Peer, a team member, went upstairs to turn the lights off. As he was making his way up the main staircase, he stopped in his tracks when he heard a man clear his throat. When he turned around, he thought he would see Ryan O'Connor standing on the staircase, holding his camera and filming him. Instead, he found he was alone in that section of the building. The team heard disembodied voices and phantom sounds of bottled wine falling over and crashing on the floor in the wine cellar. Yet upon inspection, nothing physically moved. They also witnessed TVs turned on and off by themselves. Ryan also had cameras set up throughout the location that malfunctioned; additionally, all the paranormal research team's batteries drained.

One of the investigators, Christopher Jodoin, heard movement from the dining room adjacent to the bar. As he went to see what was making the noise, he was startled by an apparition standing in the doorway to the dining room. Upon reviewing the audio files from the DVR, the team caught an EVP of a male voice saying, "It's okay, it's me, Michael."

Grill 37 has an illustrious and haunted history.

During another part of the investigation, Dan was upstairs in the office to see if any paranormal activity would happen while he was there. Team members who were monitoring the DVR saw Dan look in the vicinity of the desk. While watching the DVR live, the team witnessed a file folder turn, and it flew off the desk onto the floor. At the time, Dan, sitting in the dark, had no idea what had happened. The team tried to replicate what happened but could not.

As the team was wrapping up the night's investigation, the last camera was at the infamous table 15, which is in the old living room of the house. It was at table 15 that customers witnessed apparitions going up the main staircase and frequently asked the staff to close the door so they couldn't see the stairs. Kim Chalecki, an investigator with the team, walked up to table 15 to turn the camera and recorder off. Upon review, the team captured an amazing EVP at his location. The voice on the recorder was that of a young child crying, "I want my mommy." Perhaps this is why Nancy saw a young child wandering throughout the building. Since this finding, the child seems to have crossed over but hopefully knows he is welcome to visit anytime. The paranormal activity continues, but now that the staff knows it's just the prior residents of the location stopping by to visit, it no longer bothers them.

In fond remembrance of Nancy Atkinson, beloved manager of Grill 37, who sadly and unexpectedly passed away.

A maintenance man came to work on the interior of the building but upon arriving, became apprehensive and in a hurry to go back outside. When asked why he was so uneasy, he explained that he saw something that he knew was not a real person when he entered the building.

The ghosts are harmless and only contribute to the charm and magic of the place. Check out their website at grill37.com.

Pomfret Town House, Pomfret

The Pomfret Town House is one of three remaining original town houses in Connecticut built specifically for town meetings. The building was erected in 1840 to house meetings for all the districts of the town in one place at one time.

The Pomfret Historical Society acquired the structure and presently uses it to house exhibits and hold events, public meetings and private gatherings. Some of the members have also come in contact with the historical beings that still show up occasionally.

One member was on the small stage tidying up when he heard what sounded like someone coming out of the kitchen. Partitions were set up with

The Pomfret Town House and historical society.

pictures and papers for an exhibit, so his view of who it may have been was blocked. When he approached the partitions, he found no one behind them and no one in the kitchen. Another person working in the kitchen heard the door to the house open and close, followed by footsteps. Thinking it was a fellow member coming to help, he entered the main room but was surprised to see the door closed and the room empty of any living being.

Footsteps and voices are heard in the building, and people passing by have thought they saw a dim light like that of a candle emanating from inside the building after dark.

The Pomfret Town House in on Town House Lane, a small lane that shoots off Route 44 and then back onto it. The building is clearly visible from the highway and is available for functions when not being used for town purposes.

While You Are There: Bara-Hack, The Village of Voices

When Odell Shepard visited what he called the "village of voices" in 1927, the settlement of Bara-Hack had lain abandoned for fewer than 40 years, yet the woods had reclaimed their majesty among the foundations and ruins with breathtaking alacrity. Just having referred to the area as the village of voices denotes that it had already established a reputation for supernatural happenings.
—Connecticut Ghost Stories and Legends
by Thomas D'Agostino and Arlene Nicholson

Bara-Hack (supposedly Welsh for "breaking of bread") has been known for supernatural events since it was first settled prior to 1731. Paranormal research into the land has revealed some sort of unnatural force that occasionally brings the past into the present.

Jonathan Randall, a Rhode Island native, was active in that state's politics when he purchased 220 acres from Alexander Sessions on November 13, 1776. Randall, born on March 20, 1706, died in Pomfret in 1791 at the age of eighty-six but was buried in his hometown of Providence. Obadiah Higginbotham purchased land from John Trowbridge in 1778. Obadiah removed from Cranston, Rhode Island with his newly formed family to the woods of Pomfret sometime around 1780. He later purchased land abutting the Randall property, and what we now know as Bara-Hack came to be. Eight children were born to Obadiah and his wife, Dorcas. The whole settlement was actually two families and several servants who all lived along the old road forged between the two major properties.

Obadiah started a small spinning-wheel factory along the banks of the Nightingale Brook called Higginbotham Linen Wheels. He died in 1803 at only fifty-three years old, leaving his wife, Dorcas, to take care of the property and factory. She was forced to sell some of the land to pay debts. The factory ran until 1853. Dorcas died on July 1, 1849, at the age of one hundred. She was buried in the small cemetery that holds the remains of both the Randall and Higginbotham families.

Former owner Doris B. Townshend, who passed in 2020, wrote a book called *The Lost Village of the Higginbothams*, in which she stated that she could not find any Welsh translation of the term Bara-Hack. It does appear in Odell Shepard's book *The Harvest of a Quiet Eye*, where modern scholars seem to think the term originated. Shepard describes the area as follows:

> *Here had been their houses, represented today by a few gaping cellar holes out of which tall trees were growing; but here is the village of voices. For the place is peopled still although there is no habitation…yet there is always a hum and stir of human life. They hear the laughter of children at play. They hear the voices of mothers who have long been dust calling their children into the homes that are mere holes in the earth. They hear the snatches of song…and the rumble of wagon wheels along the old road. It is as though sounds were able in this place to get round that incomprehensible corner to pierce that mysterious soundproof wall that we call time.*

In her 1950 book *Folklore and Firesides in Pomfret, Hampton and Vicinity*, author Susan Griggs writes about the Higginbotham family and subsequent mill, referring to the area as the "Lost Village in the Hills" and never mentioning the name Bara-Hack. She does refer to the burying ground being called "God's Acre of the Hills" by the Higginbotham family. The graveyard's last internment was that of Patty Randall, who died on March 30, 1893, at the age of eighty-four years and six months. The elder Mrs. Patty Randall had died in 1809 while giving birth to her daughter, Patty.

The stories of Bara-Hack being haunted trace back at least as far as the Randall family's occupation of the property. It was recorded that the Randall family servants spied strange gremlin-like creatures the size of small children reclining among the boughs of the great elm that stood on the north face of the graveyard. The elm is long fallen, with traces of its once-majestic rule rotting just outside the burial ground's stone wall.

Cemetery at Bara-Hack, known as the Village of Voices.

In 1971, student and paranormal researcher Paul Eno investigated Bara-Hack with a small group of colleagues on three separate occasions. They heard not only voices echoing through the trees but also the barking of dogs and the lowing of cattle about them, as if livestock once again tenanted the overgrown fields. The whole group felt an overwhelming sense of depression. At one point, they witnessed a bearded face hovering over the cemetery wall for several minutes before vanishing. At dusk, orbs and blue streaks of light began to flicker about the graveyard. The group also heard children's laughter near the brook that runs through Bara-Hack.

Our personal visits to the Village of Voices were no less dramatic. While studying the names and dates within the cemetery, we suddenly heard the sound of horse's hooves and wagon wheels crunching along the gravel trail in the distance. At first, we thought it was a wagon from the nearby 4-H club passing through. The sound grew louder until it was upon us, moved past and faded down the trail. The whole occurrence lasted about one minute, yet there was no visible entity or trace that a wagon had passed by.

On another occasion, while hiking the path toward the cemetery, it felt as if the woods were alive and watching every move the living made. The laughter of children seemingly playing in the wind soon filled the air, just loud enough to hear but not loud enough to record.

As of this writing, the Wyndham Land Trust is in charge of the land, and they must clear any excursions as there are still caretakers watching over the Village of Voices, both living and otherwise.

Frog Rock, Eastford

Although not necessarily haunted, Frog Rock is a must-stop along any journey through the area. Frog Rock began its legendary history as Half-Way Rock, as it was located halfway between Ashford and Abington. From 1745 to 1800, various religious groups held open-air sermons at the rock, using it for a pulpit.

In 1880, Republican state legislator Thomas Thurber decided to paint the rock, which he passed just about every day traveling from Putnam to Hartford. Over time, the paint faded, but the rock became an icon along the side of Route 44. Soon it became a picnic stop and, as the years passed, a well-known rest area with picnic tables and, before long, a snack stand. Descendants of the families who preached at the rock saw this transformation of their sacred place as blasphemy.

Frog Rock, a destination place for many decades on Route 44.

The rock is on a small stretch of road that was once Route 44 before that section of Route 44 was moved. Frog Rock Rest Area now boasts a food stand, an antique and gift store, live music, a small playground and a wooded area to explore. There is a sign on the main road for the two-and-a-half-acre site, and yes, the glacial erratic looks just like a frog.

While You're There: Lucas Douglass, Ashford

On December 5, 1895, seventy-two-year-old Lucas Douglass was found dead on a snow-laden street in Ashford, Connecticut. He died a pauper, having never married, with few relatives. He is buried in the Westford Hill Cemetery, a small village burial ground. His plot is easy to find because it is the largest in the small burial ground. The "pauper's" grave is adorned with a thirty-four-foot-tall white Italian marble monument complete with a separate headstone surrounded by a 140-foot stone fence. Large urns adorn each corner of the wall and the entrance. A large walkway is flanked by two rows of hedges leading to the grave.

How could a man who died penniless on the streets afford such a magnificent monument worthy of any royalty? Douglass seemed very frugal during his life, saving just about every penny he earned. Shortly after he died, his will revealed specific instructions to erect the glorious memorial costing many thousands of dollars over his grave. The ornate structure is meticulously carved with columns and scrollwork topped by a great urn. One side of the monument reads, "Be thou faithful unto death." Underneath is written, "Lucas Douglass, born October 28, 1823, died December 5, 1895, aged 72 years." Above the inscriptions is a bas-relief of Douglass. Another side bears the letters "HIS" with the sentence below, "This world is not my home."

A lower section reads, "Found dead—dead and alone on a pillow of snow in a roofless street. Nobody heard his last faint moan or knew when his sad heart ceased to beat."

Above, the numerals 1, 8, 9 and 6 are intertwined. Another side has the epitaph, "Tho in paths of death I tread, with gloomy horrors overspread, my steadfast heart shall fear no ill, for thou O Lord art with me still. Thy friendly crook shall give me aid, and guide me through the dreadful shade."

The upper section is adorned with the alpha-omega symbol, which is Greek for the beginning and end. Other such inscriptions, such as "I have heard thy call," and "death is but a gentle slumber," ornament the memorial.

The massive grave of Lucas Douglass in Westford Hill Cemetery, Ashford.

Douglass selected the design, inscriptions and symbols long before he breathed his last breath. All but perhaps the inscription describing his death was his original design. This may have been an unfinished script waiting for the final moment of his life. Either way, Lucas Douglass, who passed through and from this life mostly unnoticed, knew that his last vestige of eternity would lie in the grave marker that would cover his mortal remains. Each year, hundreds of tourists travel the small country roads of Ashford to get a glimpse of the man who "died penniless" but was buried in a plot fit for a king.

The monument can be seen inside the Westford Hill Cemetery, 1796 Westford Hill Road. Please obey all rules and regulations.

Midway Restaurant and Pizza, Ashford

Want to eat where the stars ate, without the elite bill? Midway Restaurant boasts a pretty heavyweight clientele. The restaurant is located on Route 44, halfway between Providence and Hartford. A camp established by Paul Newman in 1988 called the Hole in the Wall Camp, for children with serious illnesses, sits just down the road. Newman would often visit the camp and stop by the Midway for lunch or dinner, always ordering the Greek salad and the Midway Special Pizza.

Newman often brought friends with him. Harry Belafonte, Danny Glover, Carol King and Joan Rivers were among the celebrities that refreshed themselves at the Midway. While you are there, take a moment to realize you are actually on the halfway mark between two major New England cities, and be sure to read the stories on the back of the menu.

University of Connecticut Storrs, Storrs

In 1881, Connecticut governor Hobart Bigelow signed legislation accepting Augustus Storrs's gift of a former orphanage, 170 acres of land along with outbuildings and six thousand dollars to establish what would become Storrs Agricultural School.

In 1893, its name was changed to Storrs Agricultural College, and the institution began accepting women. In 1899, the name was changed again, this time to Connecticut Agricultural College. It was not until 1934 that the college took on its famous mascot, a husky, and in 1939, it became known as the University of Connecticut.

Almost every college and university seems to hold ghostly remnants of the past, and "UConn" is no different. Several dormitories are rumored to be haunted, namely Eddy 501 and Busby 154. Residents do not say much about the exact nature of the hauntings, but the ghost of Eddy 501 is believed to be a former resident who allegedly killed himself in the dorm. People have reported feeling cold breezes even when the windows are closed and hearing knocks on the walls when no one is there. Items such as papers or posters also get torn from the walls.

A strange tale is often told about Busby 154. Whether accurate or not, here it is. Two students in the dorm heard a knock on their door. When they opened it, an early twentieth-century prosthetic limb fell in front of them. They quickly shut and locked the door, never touching the medical aid. The following day, when they awoke, the door was still secured, but the limb was inside the room. For days after, they heard weird tapping on the walls, and the microwave would turn on and beep at odd hours.

Whistling is heard in the halls, yet there is no one present to perform such sounds. Rooms 254, 354 and 444 are the most active. Then there is the New Storrs Cemetery, located on the UConn campus next to North. The seven-acre cemetery has been there since the 1860s and contains the graves of the Storrs family. Rumors circulate of it being haunted, but an old cemetery on a college campus makes situations ripe for stories.

Mansfield Hospital, Mansfield

Situated on 350 acres, the Mansfield Training School and Hospital came to be in 1917 as part of the Connecticut Colony for Epileptics. At the height of its use, the campus housed over fifty buildings and treated about 1,800 patients for afflictions. A small farm provided therapy for the patients and food for the facility.

Over time, poor conditions, allegations of abuse and neglect led to its downfall. Numerous lawsuits and concerns about the facility's poor condition forced it to close in 1993. Patients were dispersed to more modern installations throughout the state. The University of Connecticut and the Bergin Correctional Institute acquired the property and built a campus around the decaying structures. Some of the buildings were demolished, but many of them were fenced off or repurposed. The Bergin Institute is no longer there, but the Depot Campus, although strangely quiet, still thrives among the ruins and relics of the past.

In 1987, the school was added to the National Register of Historical Places. Many of the buildings still stand devoid of living souls but reportedly occupied by the spirits of those who once roamed the rooms within their

The abandoned Knight Hospital at the Mansfield Training School.

The interior of one of the buildings at the old Mansfield Training School.

walls. People investigating the old buildings have reported mists and orbs passing by the broken windows. Other experiences include the witnessing of dark shades moving about inside the buildings, strange voices and other sounds. The Knight Hospital building is where a lot of the alleged activity takes place. Much of the interior is visible through the broken windows on the upper floors.

The campus is located at the junction of Routes 32 and 44. The buildings are fenced off, and all the doors and windows are welded shut for safety. Visiting the campus is fine, but entering any of the old structures is strongly discouraged.

STONE ARCHES BED AND BREAKFAST, MANSFIELD

If you are looking for a place to stay for the night, Stone Arches Bed and Breakfast not only has first class accommodations but it also serves a great homemade breakfast with eggs fresh from the backyard chickens. Stone Arches is unique and steeped with history. Bette Day and Paul E. Stern pride themselves on their family-style hospitality and are always eager to meet new travelers. Stone Arches also has a resident ghost. In a recent email sent to the authors of this book, Bette and Paul had this to tell:

The building, originally erected by Deacon John Hall in 1694, is believed to be the oldest, or at least one of the oldest, structures in Mansfield. Its downstairs is a post and beam frame made of oak and American Chestnut. Hall, one of several brothers who settled here, was the first town clerk. The property, originally acquired from Joshua, son of Uncas, Sachem of the Mohegans, stayed in the Hall family for many generations. In the 1930s it was encased in stone, the work of a diminutive woman named Louise Ferguson. The property was written up at the time by the Hartford Courant, *which headlined the project as "Ferguson's Folly."*

Historic accounts identify at least one ghost associated with the house—a sorrowful bride named Abigail. According to the story, she was engaged to a soldier who was supposed to return to Mansfield for their wedding. On the appointed day, she put on her wedding dress and waited...and waited...and waited, only he never arrived. She was hopeful, however, and every day wore her wedding dress in anticipation of his arrival—a day that never came. She is buried across the street. Now she reportedly haunts our hallway where at least two former residents report seeing her in her flowing gown.

We have never seen her, but perhaps that's because we are too busy with our daily lives that include managing our three-room bed and breakfast and, of course, making the breakfasts for our guests. We are known for our scones—our signature dish—which we serve with every full country breakfast. We also serve fresh eggs from our fifty or so chickens. So whether our guests are here to chase spirits, attend a University of Connecticut basketball game or simply on their way to Boston or New York, we are happy to accommodate them with all the modern comforts, including a level 2 EV charging station, air conditioning and free Wi-Fi—none of which Abigail had when she lived here 200 years ago.

Stone Arches Bed and Breakfast is located at 614 Storrs Road, Mansfield Center, CT 06250. Call 860-429-2269.

While You Are There: The Green in Manchester

History buffs will enjoy taking a stroll through the Green, a historic little section of Manchester. Many of the original buildings still stand, such as the

Cone Wagon Shop, circa 1760, once owned by Ralph and Marvin Cone; the former post office; Woodbridge Farmstead; and other buildings repurposed for modern-day use. Also along the Green is a monument commemorating the site of the former Woodbridge Tavern. George Washington visited the tavern twice, once in 1781 and again in November 1789. He wrote of the place in his diary that it served "a good brand of rum."

The tavern was torn down in 1938 but is still remembered for its role in our country's founding. Thomas Hooker also passed through the neighborhood on his way across Connecticut. Route 44 takes travelers to the little neighborhood situated at the corners of Middle Turnpike East, Woodbridge and East Center Streets.

While You Are There: Nathan Hale Homestead, Coventry

Nathan Hale is Connecticut's official state hero. Everybody knows the story of how Hale became a spy for the American cause. He disguised himself as a Dutch schoolmaster, crossed enemy lines and obtained information vital to the progress of the patriot cause. Unfortunately, he was captured and hanged as a spy on September 22, 1776.

The Hale Homestead is located at 2299 South Street in Coventry. The seventeen-acre homestead adjoins the fifteen-hundred-acre Nathan Hale State Forest. Although Nathan never lived in the home that is now open for tours, a portion of the original, smaller home where he was born sits just a few yards away.

Richard Hale, a deacon and justice of the peace, built the original house in 1746. Richard married a local woman, Elizabeth Strong, and together, they had twelve children. Ten of them survived to adulthood, which, in those days, was a large number. Nathan, born in 1755, was the sixth child of nine boys and three girls. Nathan was twelve years old when his mother died giving birth to her twelfth child in 1767.

Deacon Hale met and married Abigail Cobb Adams, a wealthy woman from Canterbury. She had three teenage daughters who came to live with them. With such a large family, the small home was no longer useful. The Hale family dismantled the humble abode and built a larger one more suitable for the clan.

Much time had gone by since Deacon Hale built the home, and this passing of time had taken its toll on the old house. During this time, an incident took place that may have been one of the reasons for the haunting.

Nathan Hale Homestead.

This is Georgia F. Perry's account, as emailed to the authors, about the Nathan Hale Homestead:

Nettie Trask Works (1870–1931) was my maternal great grandmother and her sister, Fanny Trask Squires was married to Frank Squires. In an effort to avoid implication and conviction of the parties involved, the following incident was a highly secretive account of what happened one evening in what is now known as the Nathan Hale Homestead. I don't have some names and dates other than what was provided to me by my mother who passed away in 2006 at the age of 90.

Frank and Fanny were poor and didn't have any property of their own, however, for a short time they were renting what is now the Hale Homestead. According to the dates of my great grandmother's birth and death, I can assume the event must have happened in the late 1800's after the last Hale occupied the residence, and prior to the acquisition of the property in 1914 by George Seymour (1859–1945). The house was in very poor condition when Frank and Fanny occupied the house, but the rent was cheap and affordable for the Squires.

The story goes as follows: Three friends of Uncle Squires, all dirt farmers struggling to make a living, came to the homestead to play poker and drink hard cider. At some point in the evening, Frank accused one of his friends of cheating. The other two men left when the fight ensued, and were not aware that Frank had picked up the ax in the wood box, used to split kindling, and struck and killed his friend.

Aunt Fanny and Nettie were horrified at the situation. To cover Frank's crime, the women scrubbed the blood from the floor and table, and directed Frank to drag the man's body down past a big rock and into a gully along the side of the road. They buried the ax in the dirt cellar and moved some of a woodpile on top of it. Later they became more worried and moved the woodpile back, dug up the axe, burned the handle in the fire and threw the axe head into Coventry Lake.

After an exhaustive search by the police, no evidence turned up to point the finger at Frank and the case was closed. It was assumed the man was drunk, and while walking home fell into the gully and hit his head on a rock.

The story goes, that for the rest of Frank's life, if he didn't do what Aunt Fanny asked, she would threaten to turn him in. And the man that was murdered with the ax may be the ghost that inhabits the Homestead to this day.

George Dudley Seymour (1859–1945) acquired the estate and began intensive renovations of the property. Seymour was an admirer of Hale and his accomplishments. He wrote about not only the life and death of Nathan Hale and his family but also some strange accounts that occurred in the home.

The ghostly happenings began almost immediately after Seymour moved into the house. According to an account written in Seymour's journal, he and a friend traveled to Coventry to view the manor. As they arrived, they walked over to the little schoolhouse to get a glimpse inside the room Deacon Hale had built for his children. When Seymour's traveling companion peered through the pane, he came face-to-face with a man in colonial dress. The entity gave him a stern look through the panes and then vanished. The two then toured the home, and Seymour's companion let out a loud gasp when they entered Deacon Hale's old office. Displayed on the wall was a portrait of the deacon—the same face that had peered at him through the schoolhouse window.

The ghost of a former housekeeper in a long white dress wanders about the house. It has been reported that the spirit may be that of Lydia Carpenter, one of Hale's former servants. Witnesses have spied her sweeping upstairs, moving about in the kitchen, gliding down the halls and peeking around doors. The centuries have not affected her dedication to keeping the homestead tidy, as she is still very active in her toils.

People sometimes hear the rattling of chains in the cellar. This is thought to be the spirit of Joseph Hale, who died of tuberculosis—then called consumption—in the home. During the war, Joseph was imprisoned on a British ship and is somehow eternally reliving those moments in the house's cellar, rattling the chains that kept him from escaping.

Mary and George Griffith became caretakers of the house in 1930. They lived there for many years and observed countless strange incidents that could not be rationally explained. One day, Mary watched as her husband walked to the barn to milk the cows. Moments later, she heard footsteps thumping down the back stairs. She and her husband were the only occupants of the building, and no one had entered or left other than Mr. Griffith. The Griffiths believed that John, Nathan's brother, and John's wife, Sarah, may have been to blame for some of the noises in the house. The Griffiths claimed that this couple was among the spirits they encountered during their tenure at the Hale Homestead. The culprits that spooked the Griffith couple remain mysterious, like many of the haunts of the Hale Homestead.

The home was deeded to the Connecticut Landmarks Society in 1940 and is presently furnished to the exact specifications of the room's descriptions in Major John Hale's 1803 inventory, taken after his death in 1802. Both John and his wife, Sarah, died of consumption (tuberculosis) in the house.

One of the tour guides was showing the house to a family of three. The six-year-old child was misbehaving, running through the rooms and touching things. He ran into the room where the deacon's portrait hangs. The little boy came running out of the room in a panic, screaming, "There is a man in the room!" They told him it was just a painting and led him into the room to show him. The boy shook his head and said, "There was another man in here just like him, a real one." At that point, the family had to leave the house because the boy was too disturbed by the sighting.

During another tour, one of the guides heard someone upstairs and thought it was the other guide giving a tour. She called out, "Are you upstairs?" and a voice answered, "We are up here." She then proceeded to the barn, where she met the other guide. Confused about how the guide could be back at the barn so fast, she asked her who she had just guided on the house tour. The other guide answered, "I have not done a tour yet; I have been here the whole time." The only entrance to the house was in plain view of where they both stood. They both went back into the home to survey

Hale Homestead study, where Judge Hale's ghost is seen.

the situation, but no one was in there. If someone had entered or exited the building, they would have noticed.

With special thanks to the Hale Homestead, presented in the following paragraphs are some recent events that have occurred at the home.

Through the years, many of the staff have claimed to hear an audible but unclear conversation happening. There is chatter in the house, but it is indistinct.

In September 2019, two of the tour guides, Bridget and Molly, decided to conduct a quick ghost hunt with a kit they'd borrowed from the local library. After an EMF spike, they asked the question, "Do you want to communicate with us?" Later, Bridget was sitting at home listening to the recordings on her headphones and was surprised when she heard a male voice respond "Yes!" to the question.

In March 2019, at four forty-five in the morning, a photographer took a picture of the house with long exposure to capture the movement of the stars. In the picture, there is a single basement light on. When this photo was taken, the museum was closed for the season and completely vacant of the living. Even when the museum is open, the basement is rarely visited.

In the winter of 2019, site administrator Anne Marie was at the museum all day but had not been in the basement. In fact, no one had been in the basement all month. After work, she left her car in the parking lot and drove with her family to visit friends. The basement lights were on when they returned to retrieve her vehicle around midnight. Anne Marie told her family she needed to go in to see why the lights were on and turn them off. So she went into the house with her daughter, Bridget. Anne Marie got to the basement door and turned off the light. When she turned around, she found her daughter behind her, looking very pale. Her daughter explained she had heard rapid knocks from the wall beside her.

In April 2019, the Hale Homestead updated its alarm system. The technician spent the better part of the day working on the system. He finally completed the update at almost eight o'clock in the evening. Before leaving, Anne Marie, the only person left on site with the technician, asked him to wait for her outside to ensure the alarms worked. It was getting dark, and Anne Marie set the alarm and headed out. They stopped at the well so Anne Marie could sign the work order. Anne Marie was facing the house, while the technician had his back to the house. While Anne Marie was signing the paperwork, the lights in the staff kitchen turned on. She froze for a moment, then explained that they would have to go back into the house and shut off the lights. Together they went back in and did just that. The following morning, she arrived at eight thirty, and the lights were back on. She called the alarm company to ask if someone had disarmed the alarms between eight o'clock the evening before and eight thirty that morning. They verified that no one had. She also asked if the motion sensors had gone off, and the alarm company confirmed they had not.

During the summer of 2019, the air-conditioning system in the gift shop needed service. The serviceman did everything he could not to go down to the basement area to work on the air-conditioning system alone. He requested that Anne Marie accompany him while he was down there. She jokingly said, "Are you afraid to go into the basement?" Then she realized, by the look on his face, that he was! After waiting several weeks for the parts to come in, a different technician showed up. He mentioned that the first technician didn't want to come back and most technicians don't like getting calls to come to Hale Homestead because they are afraid of the basement. He admitted that the last time he was there working, he was in the basement with both sets of doors open when suddenly, the big outside doors closed one after the other, then the inside door swung slowly shut. He quickly went outside to see who might have closed the doors. There was no one around, and there was no wind whatsoever.

In August 2019, Molly went into the house to get something from a closet in the back corner. She went into the closet and let the door swing closed behind her. When she went to leave the closet, she found the door was fully closed and latched. There is no handle on the inside, so there was no way out of the closet. Eventually, another guide, Janet, found her. The door to the closet cannot latch on its own. You can swing it fast or slow, soft or hard; it does not latch on its own. Someone outside the closet has to physically lift the latch into place to close the closet. So, if Molly was the only one in this room, who closed the door behind her?

In June 2020, a volunteer was doing some work in the attic. Out of the corner of his eye, he noticed a shadow on the western side of the attic (toward the farmer's market parking field). It passed in front of the window and blocked the sun entirely for several seconds. The shadow then continued forward and disappeared.

In May 2020, Bridget was working in the garden. Site administrator Anne Marie and several other staff members were having a training session in the English barn. After a while, Bridget started to hear loud bangs from the old kitchen. The shades were down in the house, so she couldn't see what was happening inside. She assumed that the meeting was over and another staff member had started to clean the house. She continued to hear the bangs for well over an hour. As time went on, they began to get louder and move around. The banging moved into the gift shop and then back to the kitchen. Then it moved into Abigail's Hall, then the hallway, then the Judgment Room and back. Finally, she heard a very loud bang from Abigail's Hall. It sounded like someone had been standing on a chair and the chair toppled over, knocking the person to the floor. Due to the COVID-19 policies in place at the time, Bridget didn't enter the building, figuring Anne Marie would get her if there was a problem. About five minutes later, Anne Marie came from the barn into the garden. Bridget asked if she had to do with the bangs. Anne Marie was confused and explained no one had been in the house while Bridget had been in the garden. Everyone had been in the barn for their meeting, and all the doors, except the garden door, had been locked. Anne Marie, needing paperwork from her office, unlocked the door on the other side of the ell. When she entered the ell, she glanced into the eighteenth-century kitchen and saw a male figure standing there. She noticed his face was a tan color but could not see features. She entered the room, but there was no one there. Thinking back on the moment, she realized the person appeared to share space with a piece of furniture in the kitchen. If someone had been there, they could not have been standing where the cabinet is. Anne Marie and Bridget investigated the house, but it was completely vacant of any living beings.

In October 2020, on a Things That Go Bump in the Night candlelight tour, a woman saw a figure standing in the Judgment Room through the window. She couldn't identify whether it was male or female, but it was the size of an adult.

On that same night, the guests were looking through the windows of Richard's and John's Parlors. Two children, about twelve years old, were looking through the windows; the boy was looking into John's Parlor, and the girl was looking into Richard's Parlor. The children were from separate families and did not know each other. Both of them gasped and jumped back at the same time. They described seeing the exact same thing: a bluish, foggy figure of a woman who moved from John's Parlor to Richard's Parlor. The boy mentioned that she was wearing a white collar or handkerchief-like piece around her neck (a fichu). Both guides working that night were wearing colonial clothes, but neither of them was wearing a fichu.

A couple who lives in Coventry, who were on tour a different night, were surprised to learn there was no electricity in the house. They insisted that there must be some electricity in the upstairs rooms. When the guide explained there is no electricity in any of the rooms upstairs, except the attic, the couple explained that they often drove by the house at night and saw lights on in the upstairs windows of the rooms called John and Sarah's Bedchamber and the Museum Room.

Halloween night in 2020 was also the night of a blue moon. During the Bump in the Night walking tour, a man looked through the window into the Judgment Room and saw a bluish shadow figure the size of a child. It leaned into the room, pulled back out of the room and then quickly leaned in again and disappeared. The man stepped back and looked to see if it was the reflection of a child on the tour. However, the ground is sloped in front of the window, meaning it is too high for the figure to have been a reflection. The experience freaked him out. Later that night, two guides and a volunteer smelled tobacco in the front of the house (between the front door and driveway) while cleaning up from the Bump tour. They described the smell as very strong and distinct, like someone was smoking nearby. However, they were the only ones on the property. There were no other cars in the parking lots. This incident is not the only time this smell has been reported; other guides and guests have also reported smelling tobacco it at various times.

The Hale Homestead is always worth a detour to visit, whether it is for the history or the haunts.

The homestead is located at 2299 South Street, Coventry, Connecticut, 06238. Take US 44 to Richmond Road in Coventry. Stay straight onto

Sam Green Road. Bear left onto Main Street/CT 31. Turn right onto Daly Road, then right onto South Street. You may also contact the Connecticut Landmarks Society at www.ctlandmarks.org for more information.

Bolton Notch State Park, Bolton

Bolton Notch State Park was established in 1918 by the Connecticut Department of Energy and Environmental Protection. The ninety-five-acre scenic reserve was mainly formed by glacial melting and quarrying. The trails take hikers through millennia of history, from the rocky outcroppings left by the glaciers to building ruins, abandoned railroad lines now used for trails and a few caves. Twenty-six buildings once existed in the hollow, as late as 1913. Only one remains. The place was once called Quarryville but is now called Bolton Notch due to the deep trench left by the centuries of quarrying.

The Indigenous people knew the place as Saqumsketuck, meaning "a land or place of hard rock." Wiashguagwumsuck was the name given by the Podunk and Mohegans to the great flat rock found within the park at the northwestern border of the land that was thought to be sacred. Artifacts of these people have been discovered in various places throughout the reserve.

Quarrymen, a Dutchman and his wife all met untimely fates in the hollow.

The legend of the hollow and Wiashguagwumsuck begins with a Dutchman called Peter Hager who lived there with his wife, Wunneeneetmah (Wunnee), a Podunk Indian woman. They were married in the Podunk Indian tradition. One account tells that because of their interracial marriage, they were forced to live in seclusion in a small cave in the notch. When members of the local colony heard of the intermarriage, they confronted the couple, and Hager killed one of the mob—but not before he was also fatally wounded. In another account, as told in the Connecticut Federal Writer's Project, Hager was caught chopping wood on the Sabbath, a major offense at the time. The two hid in the cave to avoid arrest and whipping but were discovered. Hager shot one of the townsfolk but was also mortally wounded. He managed to make his way back to the cave, where he died. His body disappeared, and Wunnee was never seen again. Their ghosts now roam the area of the hollow where their former home, Squaw Cave, sits. A famous poem called "The Ghost of Bolton Notch" by Sue Gorton retells the story. The poem can be found on the Bolton Historical Society site. The quarry also took the lives of

Ledges at Bolton Notch State Park.

several who toiled there in the two-hundred-year history of the enterprise. Those who died there are said to remain, wandering the place where they met their untimely death.

There was once a clubhouse built by railroad executives to entertain and show off their operation at the west end of Notch Hollow. A story relates how one time long ago, four lawyers were being entertained by the company during a blizzard when a large, robust stranger suddenly entered the clubhouse and stood before the fire, warming himself. The men could not see his face, and growing suspicious that he might be a spy from a competing railroad, asked, "Where are you from, sir?"

Suddenly the room grew cold as ice. The massive figure turned toward them with eyes as red as burning coals and shouted, "From Hell, where you are going!" He then swung open the door and vanished into the swirling snow.

There is a ghost train that is occasionally seen along both the defunct and the operating tracks. The train makes no sound as its wheels move along the invisible tracks that once graced the trails. Residents near the notch have seen what resembles steam coming from a locomotive rolling down the greenway trail, as if it is once again flourishing with the railroad era. Drivers report sudden cold and mist, sometimes icing their windows as they pass over the

Old railroad tracks in Bolton Notch State Park where the ghost train is heard, now a hiking trail.

abandoned railroad line that crosses the deepest section of the notch. Many believe this is the steam from the engine of the ghost train as it passes under the bridge while motorists are traversing it.

To get to the park, look for the sign on Route 44 that takes you onto a quick exit where Routes 6, 44 and 384 intersect. This exit takes you into a parking lot. From there, grab a trail map and go.

Makens Bemont House, East Hartford

The Makens Bemont House is considered to be among the most haunted houses in Connecticut, and best of all, you can actually visit the home. The structure was built in 1761 by forty-seven-year-old Reverend Lieutenant Edmund Bemont for him, his wife and their two sons, Makens (1743–1826) and Elijah (1744–1762). Reverend Bemont lived in it just four years before Makens acquired the property with the wealth he attained in leather goods and saddle making.

The house saw much tragedy during the Bemont occupation. Makens lost his two teen sons, Elijah and Leanard, in 1799. His surviving son, Ambrose, married but lost his wife, Lovisa, in 1826. Two years later, his seven-year-old daughter, Harriet, passed into the spirit world. Ambrose remarried, and the two lived well into their eighties, dying in 1857.

The home went through several owners before the Rosenthal family purchased it. Adolph Rosenthal donated the property in 1968, allowing the East Hartford Historical Society to raise funds for its renovation. In 1971, the home was moved a half mile down the road to Martin Park, where renovations and the haunting commenced.

A man named Herman Marshall had one of the first encounters with the spirits that were jarred from their repose in the house. He had locked the door and called the security company to activate the alarms within the vacant structure. The company informed him that they could not initiate the system because there was someone in the house still hammering away at the interior. Marshall could hear the pounding over the phone, which was picked up by a microphone they had set up in the house. He went back to the building to investigate but found it completely empty. Even the operator on the other side was baffled by how the noises abruptly stopped as Marshall entered the building.

One day, Marshall heard three distinct knocks on the floor from the basement. Thinking it was a coworker needing his attention, he went down into the cellar but found no one there. Other workers heard what sounded like hammers banging away in the structure, even after they had locked up for the evening. Whatever it was, it seemed to sound like it was helping out, so the society named the "ghost" Benjamin, after the biblical translation of this name, "son of the right hand."

The house opened to the public in 1973 as the Huguenot House, although there is no record of the Bemont family ever being French Protestant. This event did not deter the spirits of the house from letting themselves be known. Banging, scratching on the walls, crashes and raps became common, unexplained noises around the house. The renovations continued well into the 1980s while the home was open to visitors. People reported being pushed by unseen hands and hearing voices and footsteps in otherwise empty areas. One ghost in particular is not shy about showing herself to the public. That ghost, always seen in a blue dress, is believed to be Abigail, wife of Edmund Bemont.

In 1982, a young girl witnessed a blue dress floating across the lawn near the house. When she looked up to see who it was, she was terrified to see that there was no physical body in the garb, which seemed to be floating on its own. Mary Dowden of the Historical Society of East Hartford had a few encounters with the spirits of the house and was not afraid to relate them. One day, she was closing the house for the season with her mother, Doris. While outside, they heard a noise from upstairs that sounded exactly like one of the old wooden windows being pulled closed. Neither of them had opened any of the windows, as it was a cold, damp day.

Mary was once giving a tour when the spinning wheel in front of the fireplace began to turn slowly. The wheel made several rotations and then reversed itself for a few turns before ceasing its rotation; this was the first time the wheel had ever moved on its own. Abigail's ghost is occasionally seen looking out the second-floor window of the children's bedroom. Although she is seen throughout the house and the yard, her ghost seems to be attracted to that particular room most of the time.

One other possible entity is thought to be the ghost of Henry James Stepanek, one of the leading volunteers in charge of restoring the old house to its former glory. The ghosts residing there are not a threat at all within the restored home that, for centuries, housed loving families and determined individuals who wanted to see the past brought back to life—perhaps more than they expected.

The Makens Bemont House is located in Martin Park with two other historic buildings owned by the Historical Society of East Hartford. The

The Huguenot House is haunted by a few former owners.

home is bounded on one side by the Burnham Blacksmith Shop (circa 1850) and on the other by the one-room Goodwin Schoolhouse (circa 1820). Martin Park is located at 307 Burnside Avenue (Route 44), East Hartford, Connecticut 06108. Take I-84 to exit 58, then Roberts Street toward Silver Lane/Burnside Avenue. Turn right onto Roberts Street, then left onto Hillside Street. Turn left onto Burnside Avenue/US 44. The home is open for tours during the summer months.

The Old State House, Hartford

The Old State House in Hartford is reported to have a few interesting ghosts roaming its corridors. Charles Bulfinch is said to be the architect who designed the structure, which was completed in 1796. It was the center of Hartford until 1873, when the modern statehouse was built. The building was declared a National Historic Landmark in 1960 and is one of the oldest remaining statehouses in the country. It is presently run by the Old State House Association and is open for self-guided tours and various events. People can also rent the building for special occasions.

When the Old State House was first ready for use, a local artist and museum keeper named Joseph Steward petitioned Governor Wolcott to have access to a third-floor chamber as an art studio. In return, he would paint portraits of famous Connecticut figures to hang on the walls of the newly appointed building. Steward also collected strange artifacts that he displayed in his studio. In time, the collection became the Museum of Natural and Other Curiosities. For a mere two bits (twenty-five cents back then), people could gaze on the horn of a unicorn or a two-headed calf along with other oddities not seen by the general populace until then. It was not long before his collection became too expansive for the cramped room in the statehouse, so he relocated the museum across the street. Steward died in 1822, and parts of his collection mysteriously disappeared, never to be seen again.

In 1975, the association created a reproduction of the museum on the second floor of the Old State House, using newspaper ads and other documents to create replicas of items Steward once displayed. They then added more items, in keeping with what they felt would have been Steward's taste. Perhaps that is why many think he is still in the old building. Footsteps are heard on the stairs going to the second level and also in the museum, which, when investigated, seems to be completely devoid of the living. Maybe Steward checks in from time to time to see what's new in his collection.

The spirit of Joseph Steward is not the only one said to be residing in the building. On May 26, 1647, forty-seven-year-old Alse Young was hanged for witchcraft in the meetinghouse square on the spot where the Old State House now sits. Alse was the first person to be executed for witchcraft in the colonies. In fact, Connecticut led the colonies in the witchcraft hysteria from 1647 to 1663. Nine to eleven accused witches were reported hanged in the Nutmeg State during this period, which ended twenty-nine years before the famous Salem witch trials of 1692. Alse's ghost is said to linger in the area, still proclaiming her innocence. Perhaps it may be one of the other accused witches wanting to clear their name. Forty-six men and women were brought up on the charge of witchcraft from 1647 to 1697; the last reported execution took place in 1663. Whoever the unidentified ghosts are that roam the sentinel walls of the historic house may be a mystery, but the museum is there, and so are some ethereal entities that seem to be taking care of it.

WEST HARTFORD TO SALISBURY, 49.29 MILES (79.32 KM)

Noah Webster House, West Hartford

While traveling through West Hartford, it might be beneficial to take a tour of the Noah Webster home. This 1790s home is where Noah Webster (October 16, 1758–May 28, 1843) was born and raised. Webster, a patriot, schoolmaster, lawyer and farmer, was responsible for printing the first American dictionary, released in 1828.

It is believed the home is haunted by Noah and his mother, Mercy Steele Webster. Visitors and staff have seen orbs floating about the garden, and a man in the basement has been witnessed; when he rounds the corner, he vanishes. It could be Noah Sr., Noah Jr. or a host of others who lived in the house after the Websters.

Locals affirm the presence of a woman in colonial garb passing by the upstairs windows. She is seen in a blue dress holding a candle. Many believe it is Noah's mother, who died in the house. A paranormal group recorded an ethereal voice calling, "Abby."

The West Hartford Historical Society, in conjunction with the Noah Webster House, holds an annual West Hartford Hauntings Tour around Halloween. It is a theatrical production taking you to the house and the North Cemetery, with guides and actors in costume telling stories of those who lived in the house and those who reside in the cemetery but may not rest. For more info, go to the Noah Webster House website.

The house is on 227 South Main Street. Go south on South Main Street after the intersection of Fern Street.

The Headless Horseman, Canton

If you happen to be traveling on Route 44 in Canton, keep your eyes open for a sight you may never forget: a headless horseman. The town of Canton was once part of Simsbury until they became separate entities in 1806. What is now Canton Village was once known as Suffrage, and it is in this village that a most bizarre and gruesome story unfolded.

The year was 1781, and the war for independence was in its final stages. French officers aiding the American armies in the field were due their pay, so a French messenger was dispatched from Hartford, Connecticut, to Saratoga, New York, with a saddlebag laden with their wages in gold and silver. The ride was long, and the horseman charged with the duty to deliver the pay was in need of a good night's rest. As the rider entered Canton, he came upon a tavern, then known as Dudley Case's Tavern, at the fork of the Albany Turnpike (Route 44) in Canton Village.

The French soldier was immediately the center of attention, clad in his fancy uniform and carrying the heavy saddlebag. He requested food and a room for the evening. After enjoying a meal and some merriment with the locals, the soldier retired to his chamber. It was the task of the innkeeper to rouse him at the break of day so that he might continue on the next leg of his journey. Unfortunately, the man was never seen or heard from again.

When the officers never received their wages, French military authorities began to retrace the route the messenger had taken. Their investigation came to a dead end at Case's tavern, where he was last seen. When questioned, the innkeeper, though a bit on edge, swore that he woke the young fellow early and saw him ride off to the west. Though suspicious, the authorities had no clues or evidence to the contrary. It was not long after that a few local youths, while enjoying some fishing in a nearby pond, found the skeletal remains of a horse and saddlebags that were at one time quite elaborate. Reservations about the innkeeper's story arose once more when it was discovered that the horse's hooves were fitted with special shoes for fast, long-distance travel.

Over time, the incident was forgotten, and the inn changed hands and became the Hosford Tavern. It was not until the Hosford Tavern burned to the ground in 1874 that the macabre truth came to light and the ghostly sightings began. The conflagration completely destroyed the old stand (an old-fashioned term for a tavern or inn) leaving nothing but its foundation. While workers were cleaning up the site, they uncovered a skeleton buried in the floor of the basement. The skeleton was complete except for the head. The skull was found several feet away in another location. It was not long after this discovery that the horrible wraith of a headless phantom horseman in a long black cape began his eternal journey along Route 44. For many years, witnesses encountered the phantom racing at a furious clip on his steed, whose eyes glowed with the fires of hell as its hooves pounded the ground, yet no sound could be heard.

After the advent of the motorcar, drivers were often taken by surprise as the ghastly specter came out of the shadows, causing them to swerve in attempt to avoid a collision. To this day, motorists still report the sudden appearance of a headless, misty figure on horseback heading west on the turnpike in the small hours of the night, their headlights shining straight through the spectral rider.

Satan's Kingdom, New Hartford

During the eighteenth century, the local clergy believed the area to be rooted in evil. Lawless bands and savages resided in the wilds, venturing out to rob law-abiding citizens or cause other mayhem. The locals were convinced that Satan also visited the area, praising his minions for their devilish deeds. Thus the name Satan's Kingdom was given to the tract of land. Over time, the lawless died off and the devil was driven from the land, but the name still describes the small recreation area where people can canoe, kayak and tube down some awesome class 3 rapids. The Tunxis Trail is marked in blue for those who prefer a nice hike. Maybe the devil may decide to sneak back onto his former property.

Satan's Kingdom can be accessed by following Route 44 west for 2.6 miles after the junction of Route 202 in Canton.

UFO, New Hartford

On July 18, 1990, in New Hartford, Connecticut, at about two o'clock in the morning, a fifty-one-year-old art history professor was lying awake in bed when she noticed bright lights flashing over her backyard. She went to the window and witnessed a small domed disc, about the size of a small automobile hovering one hundred feet away and descending over the corner of the lawn. The object maneuvered a few seconds without actually touching down. She noted that it had red, yellow and white lights that flashed sequentially around its bottom rim. It then accelerated and shot out of sight behind some trees in a second. Two days later, a hired worker asked her about some strange material on the grass. She realized it was in the area of the sighting. The National Investigations Committee on Aerial Phenomena (NICAP) investigated the site, concluding that the samples taken from the site were not consistent with natural elements.

Barkhamsted Lighthouse, Barkhamsted

The Litchfield Hills are full of amazing legends and ghost stories. The region was never overly populated and remains that way to this day. Traveling along Route 44 in this western section of Connecticut is a treat for adventurers and history buffs alike. One place that is worth a visit is the Barkhamsted Lighthouse.

A Narragansett Indian named James Chaugham, born in 1710, moved from his home of New Shoreham (Block Island), Rhode Island, to the remote territory of Wethersfield. There, he became a well-respected, hardworking young man with an affable disposition, well-liked by his neighbors.

Also in Wethersfield lived a young woman named Molly (Mary) Barber. Molly was the daughter of a wealthy businessman named Peter Barber. Chaugham met Molly and was immediately taken by her beauty and manner. Molly and James fell in love and, after a brief courtship, decided to elope and wed in secrecy. In 1740, they stole away into the wilderness, where they built a log cabin overlooking the west branch of the Farmington River. The area is now part of a 1,861-acre preserve known as People's State Forest. The cabin they erected is reported to have been the first home in Barkhamsted.

The cabin was not like any other ordinary dwelling of the time. The home was built with many windows for light and hastily chinked, so daylight entered through the cracks between the logs. The opposite took place at night when the cabin was well lit or when the Chaughams were cooking over a roaring hearth fire. The bright lights within would glow from the cabin like a beacon lighting the woods nearby, eventually giving it the name

Barkhamsted Lighthouse. James and Molly went on to have eight children—Samuel, Sally, Solomon, Meribah, Hannah Sands, Mercy, Mary (Polly) and Elizabeth—six of whom grew up, married and settled near the home where they were born and raised. Only Sally died in childhood.

People traveling the north–south trail often used the light from the house as a landmark to let them know they were on the right track and how much traveling was left before they reached New Hartford. When the Hartford-Albany Turnpike was built along the Farmington River, it passed just below the Chaugham home. Drivers of the stage heading south watched for the first sign of light from the home. When he sighted it, the driver alerted the passengers as he shouted, "Thar's Barkhamsted Lighthouse, only five miles to port!"

Native Americans, African Americans and White settlers shared the land around the lighthouse, creating a small community around the Chaugham home. The settlement grew to become Lighthouse Village. Then slowly, one by one, the citizens of the village disappeared. James died in 1790 in Riverton, while Molly, born in 1714, died on February 2, 1818, at 104 years of age. *The Barkhamsted, Conn. and Its Centennial,* written in 1881, states she died in 1820 at 105 years of age. The whereabouts of the small community was never discovered until many years later. The Barkhamsted Lighthouse sat vacant of living souls for years, abandoned to the environs of the mountain. Yet, on dark nights, travelers swore they still saw the light of a spectral fire coming from the crumbling windows of the old cabin. Many travelers accepted the ghostly glow as one of the Chaugham ghosts guiding them safely through the darkness of the wild mountain.

Sometime after 1860, the abandoned settlement became a hot spot for outlaws and other undesirables. They began to conduct their nefarious deeds in the local villages, retreating to the shelter of the abandoned village. But almost as soon as they arrived, they mysteriously vanished, never to be seen or heard from again. Tales began to circulate that perhaps the spirits of the Chaughams and their neighbors supernaturally rid the area of the lawless creatures. By the late 1800s, the area was completely desolate of the living. When the small community became an archaeological dig, at least forty graves were discovered in a burial yard near the cabin, along with the remains of ten buildings, four charcoal kilns and a common well. The *Barkhamsted Centennial* claimed that about fifty graves, all marked with crudely cut fieldstones, were actually discovered. They were reported to be those of the Chaugham family and their brethren villagers. A brass plaque marks the spot where the Barkhamsted Lighthouse once stood, but a more obvious and even more mysterious marker still entices people toward Ragged Mountain.

Deep in the woods, where the lighthouse once stood, a strange light suddenly emanates, shining brightly for all to see. On dark moonless nights, when the stars are hidden by the clouds, many claim to see what appears to be the glow of a fire beckoning them to a hearth that no longer exists, at least in this world.

The site is accessible via a short hiking trail from East River Road in Peoples State Forest and has been designated a state archaeological site.

The Winsted Wildman

According to the American Guide series, Winsted has always been known as a "never-never land where the unusual is expected to happen and usually does. Tales of five legged cows, talking owls, tame trout and even a wildman…"

The family of Caleb Beach from Winsted once had an encounter with none other than the devil. While seated to supper one evening, the family began to hear weaving sounds coming from the loom room. On investigation, they found the door flung open and a pair of fresh cloven-hoof tracks in the snow leading away from the house. *The Connecticut American Guide Series* quotes that also present was "a slight mark as if a forked tale had been drawn across the powdery surface." Gossip over the event soon turned into accusations, and not much later, a member of the parish known for his sharp tongue and less-than-pious ways was whipped for witchcraft.

One account in particular that has been told over and over for generations is that of the Winsted Wildman who terrorized the small community in the summer and autumn of 1895. On August 21, 1895, the *Hartford Courant* reprinted an article from the *Winsted Citizen* regarding an incident involving Winsted selectman Riley Smith. Smith was in Colebrook on business, and during a few moments of downtime, he witnessed something he would never forget. Smith decided to pay a visit to a place called Indian Meadow with Ned, his trusty bulldog companion. While in the field of Indian Meadow, he commenced picking and eating berries from a bush. Ned suddenly came whimpering and crawling toward him with his tail between his legs and situated himself between Smith's legs. Moments later, a creature resembling a "Wildman" over six feet tall sprang from a clump of bushes. The hairy entity let out some unidentifiable, fearful screams and cries before fleeing with lightning speed from the terrified duo.

The article stated that both Smith and his dog were paralyzed with fear despite the two being fearless and full of "pluck." In an amusing conclusion, the article went on to state if anyone had lost a wild hairy man, they could go to the Lewis Place in Colebrook and search the woods and fields in an attempt to recover their lost property.

The story spread quickly through the region and piqued the interest of newspapers in New York and Boston. Before long, Winsted was besieged by reporters, thrill seekers, ghost hunters, scientists and anyone else who might have wanted to catch a glimpse of the mysterious creature that suddenly appeared out of nowhere in the Winsted woods. Some even went as far as trying to hunt down and capture the elusive beast in hopes of bringing it to the big cities for profit. People began to pour forth with frightening stories of their encounters with the Winsted Wildman.

A certain Mrs. Mushone was in the society of one Miss Sadie Woodhouse, strolling Indian Meadow when they encountered the wildman at the same location Mr. Smith first came in contact with the monster. They described him as having large white teeth, long straggly black hair and a muscular form. The beast stood over six feet tall and was very wiry. It moved with great speed and agility as it took flight from them. Another local, James Maddrah, was also chased out of the same berry patch in Indian Meadow. He managed to shoot a picture of the wildman with his Kodak before running away.

The *Winsted Herald* reported on September 4, 1895, that A Mrs. Pulver of Colebrook, mother of Colebrook postmaster Bert Pulver, hailed a passing stage in "great distress and excitement," ranting that she had just seen the Winsted Wildman wandering around her property. She desperately pleaded with the driver to send a search party so that they might catch the wily prowler.

John G. Hall ran a stage between Winsted and Sandisfield, Massachusetts. While he was passing through Colebrook, a large creature ran out in front of him, stopping for a few moments before bounding over a stone fence and disappearing into the forest. Hall had drawn his pistol as the coach approached the creature, but the hairy beast just stood erect, staring back at the wide-eyed Hall, before making haste for the woods, accompanied by the most horrifying scream. Sightings of the Winsted Wildman spread through Norfolk, East Canaan, Colebrook, Winsted, North Goshen and Sandisfield, Massachusetts. No one in the region was safe from the possible appearance of the elusive and mysterious being.

John Williams came face-to-face with the beast while walking home one evening. Authorities were able to trace the animal's large footprints to the mountains before the trail was lost. Charles Benson of Norfolk claimed he was chased by something that jumped from a tree and pursued him at a breakneck pace all the way to his home. Farmers came forth with accounts of the wildman stealing their poultry and produce. One farmer claimed he shot at the creature but the shot bounced off its body, causing no harm or effect to it.

A group of folks from Norfolk saw the creature enter a hole in the side of a mountain. They quickly proceeded to run massive chains across the opening in an attempt to lock the monster in, but when they returned the next morning, the chains were torn asunder as if someone with great strength had effortlessly pulled the links apart.

Reporters came from everywhere for a story. After the passing of days and, in some cases, months, the reporters and prospectors left with nothing but, as the *Transcript* put it, "sunburn and hangovers from the local beer." According to one local account, a hunting party went in search of the wildman in hopes of bringing the monster back, but after following strange prints in the ground, came across a local farmer's lost donkey. A posse was formed to locate and capture the beast, but after days of searching, they, too, came home empty-handed and hungry. These failed efforts to capture the creature did not diminish the interest the Winsted Wildman had created. Newspapers still ran articles and accounts of the savage celebrity, and many theories about the identity of the elusive being were brought into the public eye.

As suddenly as the Winsted Wildman surfaced, he was gone, vanishing into thin air, never to be seen or heard from again. No one has ever put forth a rational explanation regarding the identity of the wildman. The *North Adams Transcript* ran a piece stating the creature was a large ape escaped from a circus, although no evidence turned up to substantiate that claim. To this day, the Winsted Wildman remains a ghost of sorts. He came and then vanished into legend, only to haunt the minds and pages of those who seek to know the real truth of who or what, for a short time, terrorized a region of Litchfield County.

Winchester

Winchester Center boasts a haunted burying yard called Green Lady, Greenlady's or Indian Princess Cemetery. The old graveyard sits in a remote location off an old road in the dense forest of a valley near the Waterbury Turnpike. It is there that the ghost of a young woman is often seen wandering among the gravestones in search of her lost love. Her ghost has been witnessed for almost two centuries moving about the burial ground. Because of her lengthy eternal meanderings, the ghost of Greenlady Cemetery has become one of the areas best-known legends.

When she married her local sweetheart, Mary Crocker was a young and beautiful woman. The two lived a blissful life together, but that bliss would be short-lived. A few years after they wed, the Civil War broke out, and her husband enlisted in the Union army with several other men in town. He kissed her goodbye and promised a quick and safe return.

The young husband went off to fight but was never seen or heard from again. Time went by, and Mary waited, hoping for her beloved husband's return, yet several years passed with no word or sign of her husband's whereabouts. Mary realized that he was lost for good, perhaps killed in battle and buried anonymously in some mass grave or captured by the enemy and left to rot in a prison camp. Her broken heart took her to the grave at only thirty-nine years old.

Mary was buried in the local graveyard, where her remains still lie in repose, but her soul has never rested. Her ghost is often seen wandering the burial ground, hoping to find any sign, even the gravestone, of her lost love. She is always seen in one particular corner of the cemetery where veterans of the Civil War are buried. She appears as a glowing specter of greenish hue floating sadly about the stones, hoping her love may finally return.

The cemetery is on South Road in Winchester Center.

Blackberry River Inn, Norfolk

The Blackberry River Inn's main house was erected in 1763 and underwent significant renovations in 1920. At the time, it was owned by Seth Moseley and was a working farm. In fact, the property was historically known as Moseley House Farm. After Moseley died on December 7, 1938, the property was sold to James and Dorothea Schwarzhaupt and began a new life as an inn. The property was listed on the National Register of Historic Places in 1984.

Despite its long history, the property is haunted by one lone ghost, a lady in white who has been affectionately called Frances. No one is sure if Frances lived in the house or if she was involved in the Underground Railroad. Large tunnels in the basement of the house are thought to have been part of the railroad.

Frances is often seen on the second floor of the inn, entering through the rear door of the building or walking through the backyard toward another home on the property. Her presence is by no means malicious but rather calming. She is a protective spirit whose primary eternal purpose is to watch over the inn. Those who have witnessed her ghost or felt her presence have claimed to feel an unusual calm about them. Her ghost is seen and heard often enough to make the inn the number one most haunted hotel in Connecticut, according to hauntedrooms.com.

The Blackberry River Inn is located at 538 Greenwood Road West (Route 44 West) in Norfolk.

Salisbury

Salisbury is the westernmost town in northern Connecticut. The Scoville Library, built in 1803, was the first library in the United States to be tax-supported. In 1894, it was moved to a more modern building. Another significant achievement that Salisbury can boast of is its iron mining history. Salisbury iron was sought after for many years. Now, those glory days are but a memory—but there is one thing that remains: the ghosts and the people called "Raggies."

Mount Riga Ghost Town

Mount Riga once boasted a population of over one thousand people, but by 1930, zero people remained in the once-booming iron mine town. That is, of course, if you refuse to count the ghosts and the strange people, outsiders living in the mountain wilds called Raggies.

The remains of the town now sit along Mount Riga State Park in Salisbury. Mount Riga is two thousand feet above sea level near the tristate border of New York, Massachusetts and Connecticut. Two lakes surround the thickly wooded area where the town once stood. Being on the border of the three states, the town was considered no-man's-land. Each state refused to acknowledge that the property was in its jurisdiction, leading to the area becoming a haven for lawless and questionable folk. The name Mount Riga came from the Russian immigrants who settled in the region after leaving the port city on the Baltic Sea of the same name.

Iron was discovered and mined there for almost a century. The quality of the ore was unmatched in the colonies. In fact, the town became so prominent that at one point, it had the highest per capita income in the United States and boasted the finest department store in Connecticut. Women from all around came to buy the fine silks and wares from the store. For many years, a lone apple tree marked where the great store once stood. That, too, is now a distant memory.

One of the anchors of the *Constitution* was forged in the blast furnaces at Mount Riga. The town's iron was used to produce muskets and cannons for the American Revolution and farm tools for the colonists. Unfortunately, like most towns that relied on the resources of the land for their existence, Mount Riga saw a rapid decline in population when the ore source dried up around 1847. From there, Mount Riga saw a steady decline in population.

A strange event occurred in 1802 that remains, to this day, unexplained. Some of the buildings in Sage's Ravine were bombarded by stones and projectiles that seemed to appear out of thin air. It began at ten o'clock at night on November 8, during a full moon. The phantom bombardment started with a block of wood crashing through the glass at Sage's Clothier Shop, followed by chunks of mortar. Charcoal and stone began bouncing off the building. Sage and a few others in the building rushed outside into the bright moonlit night to see where the projectiles were coming from but could find no living creature within sight of the shop. The primitive missiles just kept flying out of the darkness, causing Mr. Sage and his crew to scramble back into the safety of his shop.

By morning, the barrage of rubble had ceased, but it started up again as soon as the darkness swept over the village. The supernatural bombardment continued for three more days, each time ending well after midnight.

After about five days, Sage's shop was relieved of the phantom pelting, and Ezekiel Landon became the next victim to bear the brunt of the mysterious phenomenon. For several days and nights, Landon was beleaguered by the mystifying stone-throwing of Mount Riga. News spread, and hundreds flocked to witness the ghostly attacks. No one ever saw any sign of the stones coming from anywhere until they actually struck the side of a building or crashed through a pane of glass. Whenever a projectile hit a window, it would immediately drop onto the windowsill as if someone was placing it there. Quite often, many pieces of rock or mortar would fly through the same hole in rapid succession. It was soon concluded that the incidents were the work of witchcraft, yet the identity of the witch and the nature of the attacks continued to remain a mystery. To this day, no one has come forth with a viable explanation of the exact nature and cause of what we have come to know as the Stone-Throwing Demon of Sage's Ravine.

In time, the land became uninhabited, as the people left the area to find jobs elsewhere. The six thousand acres of land were later acquired by three families who became known as Mount Riga Incorporated. The area is now undeveloped and well overgrown, but some of the ruins are accessible via hiking trails or short walks from parking areas. The Appalachian Trail cuts through a portion of the site, and descendants of the original iron company who still own the land work with the Appalachian Mountain Club regularly to keep the trails in good condition. But very few dare to venture into the woods for fear of what lurks behind the trees.

Deep in the depths of the woods lives a group of people left over from the days of the ironworks. When the mining and forges ceased, a group of people remained behind, shunning society. As generations passed, they kept to their own, secluding themselves in the dark shadows of the mountains. Legend has it they intermarried, abiding by their own laws. This soon led to inbred families with curious features. The locals came to call them Raggies.

Few have ever seen the strange aggregation lurking among the hills. Some still exist in the forests, living on what they can. Several films have featured mutated humans living in the woods, preying on unwary hikers and travelers. The movies seem to attract adventurers to the Mount Riga area for a possible glimpse of a modern-day Raggie, but others would rather not venture into the region for fear that they might become the next meal for the strange creatures.

An old cemetery was in use when the town was populated. It is situated near the north end of Middle Road, about one-eighth of a mile from the junction of West Road. It is mostly abandoned and overgrown except for one small area where interments still mysteriously occur. There are claims that the Raggies use it to bury their deceased.

Mount Riga is indeed a ghost town, but there are a lot of untamed forests in our land that one must always use caution when exploring. You never know who or what you might meet.

Mount Riga State Park is located on Mount Riga Road, just off Route 44.

The Twin Lakes Ghost Canoe

Salisbury, Connecticut, is home to two bodies of water affectionately known as the Twin Lakes. The lakes lie about five miles from the Massachusetts and

New York State borders. The Mahican Indians of the area called the lakes Washining (Laughing Water) and Washinee (Smiling Water). They were named after a Mahican chief's twin daughters, whose tribe lived and fished along the two lakes. There is a legend of a ghost canoe that is connected to the lakes.

During a battle with a neighboring tribe, a young brave was captured and brought back to the village. The two daughters felt sympathetic toward him, as his fate was likely torture, then death. On the evening before the young brave was to meet his end, the two girls untied the young man, and the three vanished, never to be seen or heard from again. Some say that they ran off to parts unknown for fear of being found. The following day, an empty canoe was discovered floating in one of the lakes. When retrieved, the Mahicans found that it belonged to the chief.

The chief sent out many scouts to search for his lost daughters, but no sign of them could be found on land. It was soon surmised that they might have fallen overboard and drowned in the lake or that the brave, fearing recapture, killed them and stole away back to his tribe.

Since then, wanderers and visitors to the lake, especially lovers, often see an ancient canoe drifting silently in the water with no one aboard to guide it. Sometimes, what appears to be three misty figures are seen inside the canoe but suddenly vanish when the boat reaches a particular spot in the lake, perhaps where the unfortunate passengers met their fate. The ghost canoe is always seen at night when the new moon creates unnatural darkness among the stars. The ethereal canoe moves slowly and steadily, making no noise as it eternally proceeds toward a destination it never reached.

In the early 1900s, Camp Isola Bella was built on an island in Lake Washining. People camping on the island have witnessed the ghostly canoe as it silently drifts across the lake before vanishing into thin air.

Another story pertaining to the Twin Lakes is the legend of the moving stones that lie just south of Lake Washinee: large stones that seem to have pushed themselves *up* the hills of sand, forming deep trails and ruts in the hillside behind them. How they managed to perform such a feat remains a mystery. Some speculate it may be the ghosts of the lake trying to relay some sort of message, but until the mystery can be solved, the moving stones of Lake Washinee remain an enigma to all.

The Twin Lakes is north off Route 44 on Between the Lakes Road.

Leaving New England, Route 44 enters Millerton, formed in 1851 and incorporated in 1875. It is named after Sydney Miller, a railroad contractor who was responsible for bringing the railroad to the village.

CHAPTER 4
NEW YORK

MILLERTON TO KERHONKSON, 65.98 MILES (106.18 KM)
While You Are There: Dutch's Spirits, Millerton

Dutch's Spirits is an underground complex that hid a distillery during the Prohibition years. It was financed by a man named Dutch Schultz. It was the largest bootlegging operation in Dutchess County until the FBI raided it on October 10, 1932. After Prohibition, it was all but forgotten until 2010, when the owners of the four-hundred-acre Harvest Homestead Farm discovered the sprawling underground distillery. Dutch's Spirits now distills its own spirits, served with pub fare, and hosts live music, tasting events and private functions. There is one other spirit that is also present at the distillery. Some believe it is the spirit of Dutch Schultz, the man who created the operation long ago.

Both staff and visitors often get the feeling someone is watching them. There is also a heavy presence that lingers about the rooms of the facility. Some think the phantom of Mr. Schultz is still watching over his spirit operation.

Dutch's Spirits is located about eight miles from Millerton at 98 Ryan Road, Pine Plains, New York.

Amenia

Legend has it that late at night, when the moon is full, the streets of Amenia become inhabited by the ghosts of those who lived there long ago. If you should be wandering about the center of town on such a night, take heed and be aware of who you may stop and speak to.

While You Are There: Wing's Castle, Millbrook

While in the area of Amenia and Millbrook, just off the beaten path is an opportunity to stay a night or two in a castle complete with antiques and artifacts sure to raise an eyebrow. Wing's castle was the brainchild of artists Peter and Toni Ann Wing. Wing was raised on a dairy farm adjacent to where the castle now sits. The Millbrook Winery has become what was once the Wing Farm.

In 1970, the long, illustrious love affair of building a castle began. This castle is still under construction today, fifty years later. As Toni stated to the authors of this book, "It has become a live-in art project."

Stay a night and hear the rest of the story about how the idea of a castle became a home. It was all accomplished using 80 percent recycled materials!

During your stay, head down to the Millbrook Winery, just a short walk from the castle. Then jump in your car and head to the cute village of Millbrook, where you can enjoy a quiet lunch or dinner at one of the town's many great restaurants. Afterward, enjoy a stroll through Millbrook and its many antique shops.

Wing's Castle is located at 717 Bangall Road, Millbrook, New York, 12545; phone 845-677-9085. Take Shunpike off Route 44 to Bangall Road.

Note: The owners politely ask the public to please respect that this is the private residence of the Wing family, who open their home to the public during specific business hours of operation. Unless you are a guest of the B&B, there is absolutely no walking on the grounds without paid admission. Thank you.

Huguenot Street, New Paltz

Although New Paltz was founded in 1677 by Huguenot colonists, the land on which Historic Huguenot Street sits today was home to Munsee Lenape

Huguenot Street church and cemetery. *Photo courtesy of Sarah Levy, huguenotstreet.org.*

people for thousands of years prior to European contact. The town's long, complex history offers a diverse range of fascinating, eerie and macabre tales that span several centuries. Historic Huguenot Street is home to seven eighteenth-century stone houses (each with its own paranormal past), a replica Munsee wigwam, a reconstructed 1717 French church and the original Huguenot burying ground. Stories of ghostly apparitions and unsolved mysteries run rampant across the historic district.

Historic Huguenot Street now offers private one-hour Haunted Walking Tours, year-round and by appointment only. Explore the 340-year-old street with a guide who will share thrilling, eerie and mysterious tales from the darker history of New Paltz and Huguenot Street. Hear stories of past residents who lived in the stone homes and experienced terrible tragedies, encountered apparitions and held paranormal investigations.

New Paltz's history is so alive that it even comes back from the dead—from the Deyo House, where Gertrude Deyo's portrait seems to have a mind of its own, to the Jean Hasbrouck House, where a ghost named James forever remains out of guilt for not kissing his sister goodbye before she died of consumption. This tour is one hour in length. For more info, go to www. huguenotstreet.org.

The Shanley Hotel, Napanoch

Whether you begin your haunted road trip in New York State or end it there, a stay at the famous haunted Shanley Hotel should be on the agenda. The hotel has several ghosts—in fact, up to fourteen different spirits come and go as they please, no matter who is there.

Thomas Ritch erected the hotel in 1845 on Napanoch's Main Street. It was called the Mansion House. From there, the hotel changed hands several times. In 1895, a fire consumed the whole structure, but it was quickly rebuilt and open for business in no time as the Colonial Hotel. James Louis Shanley purchased the property in 1906 and added an extension to the rear of the building. This wing served as a barbershop and, later, a bordello. Shanley also added secret rooms to conceal contraband and escape tunnels in the cellar to hide from authorities. Shanley married Beatrice Rowley in 1910. The couple was well known and respected by the Irish Mob. Beatrice was close friends with Eleanor Roosevelt. In fact, it was the Roosevelts who cleared Shanley's name when he was charged with selling alcohol during Prohibition. A room was named in the Roosevelts' honor.

Tragedy struck early on as the couple had three children, but all died before reaching one year of age. Kathleen died at only five months, twenty-four days old. James Jr. died at four months, eleven days, and William passed away nine months and ten days after birth. James Sr. passed away on August 26, 1937. In 1944, the property was sold to Allen Hazen. It would change owners several more times before becoming abandoned in 1991.

In 1911, Rosie, the three-year-old daughter of the house barber, Peter Greger, fell down a well on the property across the street and died. She haunts the area of the bordello on the second floor where the Gregers resided during Peter's employment at the hotel.

Another person who is known to haunt the establishment is a man named Alfred Volkman. Volkman was executed for murdering the local preacher's nine-year-old daughter, Helen. Both he and Helen eternally reside at the Shanley.

Beatrice's sister Esther Rowley Fraughman died of influenza while living there. Her spirit resides in the room on the second floor where she took her last mortal breath. The spirit of John Powers, one of Shanley's business partners, also haunts a room on the second floor.

In 1979, a man named William Blakmur died while living at the Shanley. He may also be one of the ghosts haunting the building.

Other spirits include a man named Frank who was a bodyguard at the bordello. He met an untimely end after being shot in the pub of the hotel. A ghost named Joe and a man who whistles make frequent appearances. Several children, the ghost of a former cook and a cat named Sweet Thing are among the many ghosts haunting the property.

In 2001, the property was purchased and renovated by Salvatore Nicosia. Sadly, Salvatore passed away in 2017, and one year later, the building was once again abandoned and up for sale. It reopened under new management in 2018 and has since become a destination for paranormal enthusiasts. Connecticut Paranormal Research Team member Christine Peer worked with Sal at the hotel on weekends for eight years. She and her husband, Dan, witnessed countless paranormal phenomena.

According to Christine's account, in 1915, Dr. Walter Nelson Thayer was backing his car out of the alley between his home and the hotel and accidentally ran over a boy named Jonathan. Jonathan was taken to his third-floor room, where he died a few days later but has never left in spirit. This spirit seemed to have been attached to Christine more than the others.

Here is more of what Christine had to say about her tenure at the Shanley:

Not only are there residual haunts, most of the haunts are intelligent. Each night the occurrences guests and myself experienced would always be different. It was like the hotel was still in operation to the deceased that once visited. You never knew which spirit was going to come through and let you know they were there. I, along with several guests, have experienced seeing an apparition somewhere in the building, hearing footsteps going up and down the hallways when everyone is in one location together and seeing and hearing door knobs turning and doors opening or closing on their own. Being alone in the hotel after guests would leave, was my time to clean the rooms, changing bedding and picking up to get the hotel ready for the next set of guests coming that night. This was my quality time with the spirits. So many times, I would hear my name being called and come out of a room to see who was calling me only to find I was alone in the building. While folding laundry downstairs, I heard a ball bouncing on the staircase in the hall. I witnessed this ball come bouncing down from the third floor, around the corner onto the second floor staircase and roll into the room that I was folding laundry in. I would carry this ball back upstairs and put it back in Jonathan's room on the third floor and an hour later the ball would roll back downstairs into the room I was in. My daughters came to stay one weekend with me and during one afternoon when the guests had left, I brought them up to the third floor to give them a tour of some of the rooms. As soon as we got to Jonathan's room, clear as day, we heard a little boy tell them, "Don't be scared, come in and play." Of course, my girls at the time got scared and ran back downstairs. Later, they asked to buy him some toys so they could give them to him. Guest would also bring toys for Jonathan and Rosie.

We have heard so many ghostly encounters from thousands of guests each morning after their stay as we would sit around drinking coffee and having breakfast with everyone over the years. The Shanley Hotel is a place we highly encourage to visit if you're into the paranormal. Since Sal's passing in 2017, the hotel was purchased by new owners who are continuing the restoration in which they have done major improvements to this beautiful hotel. We will continue to visit what I once called my second home and look forward each time to the restorations being made. So, feel free to book a night at The Shanley Hotel and step back into time to experience the history of this location for yourself.

The hotel has thirty-five rooms, secret passages, a basement, an attic and plenty of ghosts. Guests can bring their own ghost-hunting equipment, or it is furnished for use and also available for purchase in the gift shop. No weapons or alcohol are allowed on the premises. For more information and booking, go to www.thehauntedshanleyhotel.com.

Dutchess County Community College, Poughkeepsie

Dutchess County Community College sits on 130 acres of land with eleven buildings offering sixty-degree certificate and microcredential programs in subjects ranging from aviation to performing arts. There are many interesting clubs to join, and the campus is state of the art and beautiful. There is even one building on campus that boasts a ghost.

Bowne Hall, built in 1913, is the oldest building on campus. It began its life as the Netty Bowne Hospital before being acquired by the community college. Extensive renovations were made in order to house administrative offices, classrooms and a conference space. The renovations may have stirred a few sleeping spirits. Staff and students have reported a strange presence wandering the halls of Bowne. No one knows for sure who the spirit or spirits are, but they are definitely felt within the building.

Christ Episcopal Churchyard, Poughkeepsie

Just a few thousand yards south of Route 44 sits the Christ Episcopal Church, an established church since the 1760s. The church received a royal charter in 1773. When the War for Independence broke out, tensions between Reverend John Beardsley and his congregation caused Beardsley, a British loyalist, to abandon his parish and move to New York City.

The first church was erected at the corner of Market and Church Streets but was later replaced with a more modern structure in 1834. The present church was erected between 1888 and 1889 on a plot of land that was once known as the English Burying Ground. When the church acquired the property, it commenced moving the graves of both the English Burying Ground and the old churchyard on Market Street to the Poughkeepsie Rural Cemetery. Family members also had the option to take their loved ones' remains for private burial elsewhere. Somewhere during this transition, not all the graves may have been moved.

The church is reportedly haunted by a woman who suddenly appears in an empty pew during services. A former pastor's ghost is also said to remain behind, watching over his church. The pastor died in the 1940s. Shadow figures and other apparitions occasionally appear inside the building. There are even reports of a decapitated head floating among the pews and maniacal disembodied laughter that echoes throughout the building. The spirits' identities remain a mystery, but church records may help shed some light on the subject.

Elijah Willoughby died in 1829 after a brief but brutal illness. He was buried in the English Burying Ground before being removed to the Rural Cemetery. A monument on Christ Church Square states he died in 1827. Perhaps he is disgruntled over the error. John Phelps was one of the 2,100 Union soldiers killed at the Battle of Sharpsburg, also known as Antietam. He may be another lingering entity. An unknown youth about nineteen years old was killed on the railroad tracks and buried in the churchyard. He may very well be one of the ghosts lurking about the church.

The church is located at 20 Carroll Street. Visitors are welcome to attend services. You can even subscribe to the church's newsletter to keep up with the latest events and services.

While You Are There: Poughkeepsie Rural Cemetery

The cemetery was established in 1853 and spans forty-three acres. It is haunted by several ghosts, perhaps a few that were moved from the English Burial Ground and the churchyard on Market Street when the Christ Episcopal Church moved from one place to the other. One ghost in particular is a dark-haired woman in a white dress, perhaps a burial shroud, seen moving among the gravestones. People visiting the cemetery, walking by or driving past have witnessed her glowing apparition near the road.

Other apparitions have been reported in various sections of the cemetery along with shadow figures, sudden cold spots and the feeling of being watched while meandering through the burial ground. The cemetery is located at 342 South Avenue in Poughkeepsie. Please obey all rules and regulations.

Miss Fanny's Victorian Party House, Wappingers Falls

New York State boasts some of the more interesting haunted places to stay and investigate. One such place is Miss Fanny's Victorian Party House south of Route 44 at 4 Van Wyck Lane in Wappingers Falls. Miss Fanny's is a three-story farmhouse built circa 1860–70, named after the last of the family line to inhabit it. The home has been featured on several paranormal shows because of its constant ghostly activity.

The spirits residing in the house like to open and close doors and walk around the place; footsteps are often heard where there is no human to perpetuate them. Voices are heard coming from otherwise empty rooms and halls, and full-body apparitions have even appeared in front of guests. During an investigation, the door to the "haunted bathroom" tore open with such a velocity that it actually pushed past the point in the floor where, due to age, it usually stops and needs extra assistance to open.

Miss Fanny's is available for weddings, showers, overnight stays, paranormal group investigations, photo shoots, etc. You name it, and they will try to accommodate it. Visit www.missfannys.com.

FDR Mansion, Hyde Park

While visiting Poughkeepsie, historians and mansion buffs might want to pay a visit to the home of Franklin D. Roosevelt in Hyde Park. The Springwood estate was the birthplace, home and burial place of the thirty-second president of the United States. Roosevelt was the longest-serving president in the history of the United States. Guests have claimed the mansion is haunted with a cold feeling in places and a sad feeling in the dining room and Mrs. Roosevelt's bedroom. Tours are available for a fee. This 1945 National Historic Site at 4097 Albany Post Road has a lot to see and do. You never know what you will experience.

BIBLIOGRAPHY

American Guide Series Federal Writers' Project. *Connecticut: A Guide to Its Roads, Lore and People.* Boston: Houghton Mifflin, 1938.

———. *Massachusetts: A Guide to Its Places and People.* Boston: Houghton Mifflin, 1937.

———. *Rhode Island: A Guide to the Smallest State.* Boston: Houghton Mifflin, 1937.

Balzano, Christopher. *Dark Woods: Cults, Crime, and Paranormal in the Freetown State Forest.* Atglen, PA: Schiffer, 2008.

———. *Ghosts of the Bridgewater Triangle.* Atglen, PA: Schiffer, 2008.

Bartholomew, Robert E., and Paul B. Bartholomew. *Bigfoot Encounters in New York and New England.* Surrey, BC: Hancock House, 2008.

Bowden, Mary Grant. *Journey through New England: A Guide.* Boston: self-published, 1970.

Bromley, Seth. *A Real Ghost Story.* Cumberland, RI: Northwest Neighbors, October 31, 2003.

Cano, Deborah, T.J. Heroux and Marie Terrien. *Ghost Stories and Urban Legends of New England.* Montgomery, AL: E-Book Time, 2008.

Citro, Joseph. *Weird New England.* New York: Sterling, 2005.

DePold, Hans. *Bolton Horizons.* February 2010. Self-published

Dunn, Richard S., and Laetitia Yeandle. *The Journal of John Winthrop 1630–1649.* Cambridge, MA: Harvard University Press, 1996.

Fisher, Jeffery. *Ghosts of Connecticut and Rhode Island.* Kindle ed. Self-published, n.d.

Flad, Mary. *A Church in the City.* Poughkeepsie, NY: Christ Episcopal Church, 2016.

Flagg, Ruth H. *Phineas Gardner Wright: The Man and His Monument.* Putnam, CT: Aspinock Historical Society, 1995.

Gellerman, Bruce, and Erik Sherman. *Massachusetts Curiosities: Quirky Characters, Roadside Oddities, and Other Offbeat Stuff.* Guilford, CT: Globe Pequot, 2004.

Guild, Reuben Aldridge. *Early History of Brown University, Including the life, Times, and Correspondence of President Manning. 1756–1791.* Providence: Snow & Farnham, 1897.

Haunted Rooms. "The 6 Most Haunted Hotels in Connecticut." Last updated February 25, 2022. https://www.hauntedrooms.com/connecticut/haunted-places/haunted-hotels/.

Holzer, Hans. *Yankee Ghosts.* Dublin, NH: Yankee Publishing, 1986.

Ignasher, Jim. *Forgotten Tales of Rhode Island.* Charleston, SC: The History Press, 2008.

———. *Remembering Smithfield: Sketches of Apple Valley.* Charleston, SC: The History Press, 2009.

———. *Smithfield's Lost City: The Story of Hanton City and Its People.* Smithfield, RI: self-published, 2005.

Lee, Darcy. *Ghosts of Plymouth, Massachusetts.* Charleston, SC: The History Press, 2017.

Lee, Wallace. *Barkhamsted, Conn. and Its Centennial.* Meriden, CT: Republican Steam Print, 1881.

Lodi, Edward. *Haunters of the Dusk.* Middleborough, MA: Rock Village Publishing, 2001.

———. *Shapes That Haunt New England.* Middleborough, MA: Rock Village Publishing, 2000.

McCaffery, Jen. "Haunted Yes; Dangerous, No." RI Monthly.com, February, 2012.

MUFON UFO Journal, December 1990. MUFON (Mutual UFO Network). https://mufon.com/

National Park Service. "The Tree Root That Ate Roger Williams." October 19, 2015. https://www.nps.gov/rowi/learn/news/the-tree-root-that-ate-roger-williams.htm.

Parsons, Usher. *Indian names of Places In Rhode Island.* Providence: Knowles, Anthony, 1861.

Pitkin, David. *Ghosts of the Northeast.* Salem, NY: Aurora Publications, 2002.

Platt, Jim. "The Ghost Train." *Pomfret Times* 24, no. 5 (August 2018).

Plumb, Taryn. *New England UFOs: Sightings, Abductions and Other Strange Phenomena.* Guilford, CT: Down East Books, 2019.

Reynolds, Helen Wilkinson. *The Records of Christ Church Poughkeepsie, New York, Vol 2.* Poughkeepsie: F.B. Howard, 1917.

Rhode Island School of Design. "History and Tradition." https://www.risd.edu/about/history-and-tradition.

Robinson, Charles Turek. *The New England Ghost Files.* North Attleborough, MA: Covered Bridge Press, 1994.

———. *True New England Mysteries, Ghosts, Crimes, Oddities.* North Attleborough, MA: Covered Bridge Press, 1997.

Robinson, William. *Abandoned New England: Its Hidden Ruins and Where to Find Them.* Boston: NY Graphic Society, 1976.

Smitten, Susan. *Ghost Stories of New England.* Edmonton, AB: Ghost House Books, 2003.

Steiger, Brad. *Project Blue Book.* New York: Ballantine Books, 1976.

Tanner, M.O. "Exploring 'The Rumbly.'" *Observer* 17, no. 13 (May 1972).

———. "Hanton City Revisited." *Observer* 17, no. 24 (August 1972).

Weston, Thomas. *History of the Town of Middleboro Massachusetts 1699–1905.* Boston: Houghton, Mifflin, 1906.

White, Glenn E. *Folk Tales of Connecticut.* Meriden, CT: Journal Press, 1977.

———. *Folk Tales of Connecticut Volume 2.* Meriden CT: Journal Press, 1981.

Websites

Gatehousemedia.com.

Haunted History Trail of New York State. https://hauntedhistorytrail.com.

Haunted Places. https://www.hauntedplaces.org

Haunted Shanley Hotel. https://thehauntedshanleyhotel.com.

Historic Huguenot Street. https://www.huguenotstreet.org.

Internet Archive. https://archive.org.

MUFON (Mutual UFO Network). https://mufon.com/

National Investigations Committee on Aerial Phenomena. http://www.nicap.org/.

Roadtrippers. https://roadtrippers.com.

Shadowlands.net.

Strange Maine. http://strangemaine.blogspot.com.

Wikipedia. https://www.wikipedia.org.

ABOUT THE AUTHORS

Tom and Arlene are ardent researchers of New England history, haunts, legends and folklore. Creators of fourteen books, together they have penned and captured on film the best haunts and history New England has to offer. Tom has contributed to various other books and publications and has appeared on many television and radio shows, as well as documentaries on the subject of the paranormal. Arlene is a professional photographer with a degree in photography. Tom is a graduate of Rhode Island College with a degree in political science. He is a professional teacher and musician. Tom builds his own musical instruments, many from the Medieval and Renaissance periods, that are used in his profession.

FREE eBOOK OFFER

Scan the QR code below, enter your e-mail address and get our original Haunted America compilation eBook delivered straight to your inbox for free.

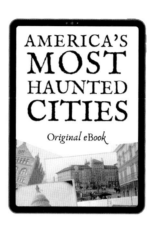

ABOUT THE BOOK

Every city, town, parish, community and school has their own paranormal history. Whether they are spirits caught in the Bardo, ancestors checking on their descendants, restless souls sending a message or simply spectral troublemakers, ghosts have been part of the human tradition from the beginning of time.

In this book, we feature a collection of stories from five of America's most haunted cities: Baltimore, Chicago, Galveston, New Orleans and Washington, D.C.

SCAN TO GET
AMERICA'S MOST HAUNTED CITIES

Having trouble scanning? Go to:
biz.arcadiapublishing.com/americas-most-haunted-cities